Cover Photo: The Shuttleworth Collection's Blackburn Monoplane (1912) Type D, photographed by Clement Allen

ISBN: 1-53066-384-9
ISBN 13: 978-1530-66384-2
Library of Congress Control Number: 2016905048
CreateSpace Independent Pub Platform, North Charleston, SC

AEROPLANES:

A Compilation of the World's Original Aircraft Built Before 1920

Michael A. Antonelli

Contents

United States of America

Acknowledgments

Thanks need to go to all those who raise their hands and proactively inform the general public of what artifacts they possess. This information comes with a great deal of detail as to how they acquired the treasure, but more often than not, little is known about the provenance of specific antiques.

The effort of the curators and staff members of many museums all around the world cannot go without grateful recognition. This author has enjoyed an outpouring of replies to some very specific information requests. For this, the project can only be called a team effort.

To be fair to all who have attempted a compilation like this in the past, know that with each passing year the internet has made a project such as this far easier than before. With tools like Google Translate and other similar programs, the process of understanding languages is possible, although time-consuming. At least twenty languages were used in this book. Special thanks go to all of those organizations outside of the United States who answered my questions sent to them in English.

Introduction

It has been more than one hundred years of manned, powered flight. The lion's share of the advancement came during the years 1914–1918, as a world war raged and the need for rapid advancement in battle technology became the priority.

In compiling a record of the "surviving" original aircraft, the years before 1920 were chosen simply because this era is the dawn of aviation defined by all those whose experiments led eventually to sustained powered flight, accomplished by the Wright brothers in 1903. The end of hostilities in World War I came about in 1918, but many original aircraft exist today that were designed with the Great War in mind but were built after the Treaty of Versailles was signed. It seems inappropriate to exclude original aircraft preserved today that were not built within an overly stringent time period such as 1903–1918. However, all compilations need guidelines, and 1920 was loosely chosen as a cutoff, although there are exceptions within the book, with build dates after 1920 in some cases, because these examples document a popular war example.

Early aircraft survivors are found in abundance in the United States, but truth be told, there are originals found across the globe on all seven continents. Yes, even in Antarctica. The world has become much smaller, and with prize pieces of aviation collections changing hands across countries (e.g., from the United States to New Zealand), an attempt has been made to list *all* known survivors around the world.

Many specific survivors found throughout the world are detailed here. These were chosen as good examples that are not frequently written about. There are varying degrees of information or provenance about these specific aircraft. It is hoped that the readers of this book will contribute more details, recommend revisions, and bluntly point out inaccuracies, which are inevitable when pursuing many sources across continents.

Accuracy in any compilation is always a concern. Attempts have been made to hold accuracy as the most important guideline. A great deal of research has been contributed over several years here, and it is hoped that this compilation will only act as a starting point for establishing a consistently updated list of original early aircraft, their location, and their movements. The author fully expects readers to have information that will improve the details of this listing and welcomes correspondence so as to achieve the most accurate and complete compilation possible. Please feel free to reach out to the author at antonelli_michael@yahoo.com.

In the case of such popular (many in existence) aircraft such as the Standard J-1, the Curtiss Jenny, and the Thomas Morse Scout, for example, some will simply not be documented and therefore remain unknown to the public, resulting in a less-than-complete listing. It is hoped that in future editions many of these quietly owned originals will stand up and be counted, allowing for all original owners to become a true community. Interestingly, many of the finest museums in the world do not necessarily list/detail some of the original aircraft they possess. This most often occurs when the specific artifact is being restored, in storage, or simply not viewable by the public.

A few words about China: It is hard for this author to believe that, in this expansive country with such a rich history, there can be found no known original early aircraft. We know that the Chinese purchased at least twelve Caudron aircraft during World War I, but none seem to have survived. It also seems that Feng Ru, who was

China's first airplane designer and builder and who earned China's first pilot's certification in 1909, owned at least two aircraft, neither of which exist today.

Purpose of Compilation

Aviation as art: There is a fascination with early aeroplanes (the word first used to describe what we now call airplanes), not necessarily because they seem so precarious to fly, but because, in an effort to stay light, they maintain an artistic beauty in their construction. Wood and wire, cloth and castor oil—early aircraft utilized some aluminum, but composites could only be imagined. Often, in an effort to emulate birds, aeroplanes were built as mechanical reproductions of something only nature could create.

Although the armistice of November 11, 1918, ended the fighting, the Treaty of Versailles formally ended World War 1 on June 28, 1919, five years to the day after the assassination of the Archduke Ferdinand and his wife, the unofficial start date of the war. One of the main provisions of the treaty was for Germany and her allies to accept full responsibility for the losses and damage caused by the Great War. By doing this Germany was forced to eliminate their air force, called the Luftstreitkrafte, and systematically destroy much of their war machine, including aircraft. This is why original Axis aircraft are rare, especially multiengine bombers.

This begs the question of how even these aircraft still exist if, by treaty, they were to be destroyed. The answer lies in the concept of "the spoils of war." Most surviving Axis aircraft were gifts or war trophies presented to various countries and organizations. Even some of the few early German aircraft that sidestepped the rules of the treaty were later destroyed in World War II. The best example of this was the destruction of the last Fokker Triplane (DR.1), lost in the bombing of the Zeughaus Museum in Berlin by the Allies during the war.

The Order of Things

This book focuses on early aircraft originals, sometimes referred to as "survivors" throughout the world. There are approximately 550 early original aircraft (1920 and prior) in existence in the world today. The museums/collections that contain survivors are all listed in alphabetical order with a hierarchy that is broken out by

- continent;
- country (United States museums/collection are broken out by state);
- city; and
- museum/collection/private owner.

Every attempt has been made to document provenance for individual featured aircraft; however, in the many cases where little is known about the history of a plane, only what is considered factual has been noted. This book has stayed away from making assumptions that may be incorrect. When documenting provenance, sometimes less is more.

The list attempts to be all-inclusive but does not detail replicas or reproductions. It seems that, over the years, the definitions of *replica*, *reproduction*, and *original*, depending on whom you speak to and where they are from (museum, organization, etc.) can vary. For this publication, and with the assistance of the TIGHAR organization's manual, they will be described as follows:

- A *reproduction* is defined as a precise copy of an existing aircraft, often using original plans and incorporating original parts.
- A *replica* is defined as an object constructed to represent, to a greater or lesser degree of accuracy, an aircraft that existed at some previous time.
- An *original* aircraft is defined as the actual aircraft that is passed down from a particular time in history. The aircraft has provenance and maintains a manufacturer's serial number. While this seems straightforward, many originals have varying degrees of original parts, fabric, armament, engines, and so forth.

This book covers the aircraft that are generally considered by most to be original, whether by documented serial number or by the impressive proportion of original parts. In some cases, aircraft are presented in the compilation that are amalgamations of several original parts or sections of surviving aircraft. These are listed in most cases, and there will be a few examples in this list that are not officially considered original but have been included to allow this book to remain as comprehensive as possible. The reader is invited to make the final determination of "originality worthiness" himself.

Note: TIGHAR (pronounced "tiger") is the acronym for the International Group for Historic Aircraft Recovery, a nonprofit foundation dedicated to promoting responsible aviation archaeology and historic preservation. The foundation devotes its resources to saving historic aircraft wherever they may be found and to educating the international public in the need to preserve the relics of the history of flight.

Part One: Some of the Finest Survivors

Grigorovich M-5

[Istanbul Aviation Museum in Istanbul, Turkey]

Istanbul, Turkey, still known as Constantinople during World War I (and as Byzantium thousands of years before the Great War) is a mecca for antiquities. But perhaps to the surprise of some, Istanbul is also home to an aviation museum that houses an impressive collection of aircraft engines. Alongside these power plants is a rare and apparently original Grigorovich M-5.

As the story goes, the Istanbul Aviation Museum was first conceived at the end of hostilities in 1918 simply because German aircraft existed as war booty. Unfortunately, many of these aircraft were wrecked in the process of moving them from place to place over several years. Ironically, part of this moving process was a result of trying to protect these veteran aircraft from damage during Turkey's War for Independence fought from 1919 to 1923.

The Grigorovich M-5, sometimes referred to as a Shchetinin M-5, was a large flying boat used mostly for reconnaissance. The M stood for marine. This Russian-built aircraft was first seen in the skies (and the water) in 1915. Manufactured by Shchetinin, the first Russian aviation company, established in 1909 by pilot S. S. Shchetinin, the M-5 was designed by Shchetinin's lead designer, Dmitry Pavlovich Grigorovich. As is the case with almost all early flying boats of this era, the M-5 copied heavily from the successful Curtiss designs. The Curtiss Model Ks used by the Russians had the distinct disadvantage of having to be shipped from the United States in crates through several ports. Many arrived with cracked hulls and therefore were unable to float.

Designer Grigorovich studied at the famous Kiev Polytechnic Institute, where he fostered his interest in flying boats. However, Kiev is not the ideal place for building and flying the designs Grigorovich had penciled, so he moved in 1911 to Saint Petersburg. It was here that Sergei Shchetinin saw Grigorovich's first aircraft. This first Grigorovich aircraft was not a flying boat, for which he would eventually become famous. Instead, it was a land-based contraption. Sergei wasted little time in offering Dimitry a job at the Shchetinin Company as manager and technical director of the plant.

At a time when few could imagine the true uses for the aeroplane, Grigorovich had a good sense of the possible use of aircraft in war. He was given the opportunity to work on and repair early foreign aircraft—namely, the French hydroplane "Donnet Leveque"—and he made aerodynamic improvements that led to his first manufactured design, the M-1. The M-1's airfoil provided greatly improved lift characteristics from water, and the aircraft saw its first flight in June 1914, just two months before the outbreak of World War I.

Later, improved and constructed out of wood with wings and tailplane covered in fabric, the new M-5 sported a 7.62 mm Vickers machine gun mounted out in front of the hull. Despite having to rise out of water, the M-5 could carry 660 pounds of cargo. Most M-5s had a 100-horsepower Gnome Monosoupape engine in a pusher configuration, but some had 110-horsepower LeRhone or 130-horsepower Clerget engines installed. The original in the Istanbul Aviation Museum has the Gnome.

The Istanbul Aviation Museum's M-5 was a Russian navy example that was forced to make an emergency landing in Turkey and seized by the Ottoman Empire.

Vickers Vimy

[Smith Brothers Memorial in Adelaide, Australia]

The Vickers Vimy was introduced in 1919, which one has to admit is slightly outside the date range this book has been attempting to adhere to. However, when it comes to the Vimy and its history for breaking early aviation records, we couldn't help ourselves.

Designed for World War I but built after the hostilities, the Vickers Vimy was a British-made heavy bomber that was designed for night raids deep into Germany. The name Vimy comes from the famous battle of Vimy Ridge, in which the Canadian Corps, made up of four divisions, battled three divisions of Germany's Sixth Army. In mid-April 1917, the Canadians succeeded in beating back the Germans who, at the time, controlled the high ground. The battle of Vimy Ridge was essentially part of the bigger Battle for Arras.

The Vickers Vimy was a twin-engine aircraft that incorporated the Rolls Royce Eagle VIII engine for those that were delivered to the RAF. Military use of the type came as the Vimy was used as the frontline bomber in the Middle East from 1919 to 1925. It was also used as a trainer and continued to see use into the late 1930s as a target aircraft.

Seen today within a specially built memorial building in Adelaide, Australia, is Vimy G-EA-OU or more specifically, serial number F8630. This aircraft is memorialized due to the incredible first flight achievement by the Smith brothers (Keith and Ross), who flew from England to Australia in 1919 in this actual aircraft. This flight came about when it was decided that aviation in Australia could use a boost. The Australian prime minister at the time, the Honorable Billy Hughes, offered a commonwealth government prize of £10,000 to the first Australians to fly from England to Australia in fewer than thirty days.

The Smith brothers, who were eventually knighted for their success, flew this distance in twenty-eight days. Interestingly, it was calculated that if relay teams were maintained (aircraft, crews, etc.), flying from England to Australia could take as little as five days. It took an incredible twenty-five years after this flight for this trip by civilians to become a real travel option.

Vimy G-EA-OU was owned by the Australian War Memorial, where in 1958 it was moved to its present hangar in Adelaide. It is a Vickers F.B.27A type IV Vimy with the RR Eagle engines and altered with additional fuel capacity.

The most famous Vickers Vimy is today found in the Science Museum in London. John Alcock and Arthur Whitten Brown made the first nonstop crossing of the Atlantic in June 1919 in that aircraft. (Charles Lindbergh achieved this same distinction with much greater fame years later, because he did it alone). Alcock and Brown left Newfoundland on June 15, 1919, and landed at Clifden in Connemara, Ireland, sixteen hours later.

Yet another Vimy achievement (actually, more of a partial Vimy success) was the 1920 flight of pilots Lieutenant Colonel Pierre van Ryneveld and Major Quintin Brand. They attempted to make the first flight from England to South Africa. But ultimately, they needed to finish the flight by using a second Vimy and then switching yet again to an Airco DH.9. The two left Brooklands, United Kingdom, on February 4, 1920, in Vimy

G-UABA, named *Silver Queen*. The first stretch ended well, with a safe landing in Heliopolis, but the next stage to Wadi Halfa ended in a forced landing, due to an engine problem, with just eighty miles left. This is where a second Vimy was borrowed from the RAF. Named *Silver Queen II*, this second aircraft continued to Bulawayo in Southern Rhodesia, where it was wrecked on takeoff. Van Ryneveld and Brand were granted yet another favor, as they received a South African Air Force Airco DH.9 to continue the journey to Cape Town. On their arrival, the two pilots were awarded £5,000 each by the government of South Africa.

Vickers Vimy—Smith Brothers Memorial

4

Avro 504K

[Australian War Memorial in Canberra, Australia]

Opened in 1941, the Australian War Memorial is a national tribute to all those who participated in the armed forces of Australia. It is quite literally a memorial to the more than one hundred thousand Australian soldiers, men and women, who have died serving in the conflicts of the Australian nation. Housed within are the relics of these conflicts from world wars and regional conflicts to peacekeeping efforts throughout the relatively brief history of Australia.

The rich history of Australian participation in World War I is well known, not just for battles such as Gallipoli but for involvement in Egypt and later in Europe on the front. The Australian Flying Corps (AFC) was formed in March 1914, and it was sent to German New Guinea with one BE2c aircraft and crew. The AFC saw action in Egypt as it expanded eventually to be made up of four squadrons. It was not long after the war when the AFC became the Australian Air Corps and ultimately in 1921, the Australian Air Force.

The Avro 504K was used as a trainer, and it was in this role that it served with the AFC, starting in 1915. Alongside the four already operational squadrons, four training squadrons—the fifth, sixth, seventh, and eighth—were established. Based in the United Kingdom, the AFC squadrons used the 504K as their primary training aircraft.

The name Avro was derived from the name of the founder, Alliot Verdon Roe, in 1910. A. V. Roe first developed the Roe I Biplane in 1907. And with the help of his brother, H. V. Roe, who was a successful businessman, he built the Avro name into a trusted aircraft manufacturer just in time for World War I. The Avro 504K was built in large numbers with some participating in the war but an even larger number playing important roles after the war. A very large number were built, approximately eighty-three hundred, with only about eleven originals in existence today. Avro can thank the RAF for its success, as the 504K became the staple for all flight-training activities.

As is the case of most trainers, the Avro 504K is a two-seater powered by a 130-horsepower rotary engine. The airframe is built of wood, with the fuselage, wings, and tail all covered in fabric. The fuselage is wire braced and has four longerons. The aircraft was designed to accommodate Clerget, Le Rhone, and Gnome engines. The two cockpits host a set of instruments that only vary in complexity. The front panel has many instruments and most of the "bells and whistles," while the second panel in the back cockpit has only basic instrumentation.

Quite distinctive to the Avro 504K is the undercarriage, which consists of a steel tube frame with wire bracing. This frame supports a long wooden landing skid and a pair of Palmer Cord aircraft wheels. The wheels have wire spokes and are fitted with circular fabric covers.

The Australian War Memorial has Avro 504K with serial number H2174 (later A3–4). Purchased in 1918 by the AFC as part of a bigger order of twenty other aircraft, it was shipped to Australia from the United Kingdom damaged. Consequently, records show that it wasn't until 1920 that H2174 saw service. At first it was used in Eastern Australia as part of the "Second Peace Loan" flights (a savings bond sales effort for returning World War I vets). Later, in 1921, the now-renamed the Royal Australian Air

Force or RAAF, used this Avro 504K as a trainer at the flying school in Richmond. The 504 remained there until 1927, when it was donated to the memorial and exhibited in Melbourne until 1941, when it was sent to Canberra where it remained until 1955. At this point it was taken apart and placed into storage until Qantas (the airline of Australia) borrowed the Avro so as to create two replicas. While the memorial's original was in their hands, Qantas restored the original.

Avro 504K—Australian War Memorial

Pfalz D.XII

[Australian War Memorial in Canberra, Australia]

The AMW, located in Canberra, is made up of three distinct sections: the commemorative shrine, which contains the Tomb of the Unknown Australian Soldier; the Galleries, which house one of the finest military museums in the world, and the Research Center, which maintains historic records.

Within the Galleries there is ANZAC Hall, which is a large annex to the upper level of the memorial used to display large military hardware, including aircraft. ANZAC is the acronym for Australian and New Zealand Army Corps, which was formed in 1915. You'll find a Lancaster bomber, a Japanese Ko-hyoteki class midget submarine sunk during a raid on Sydney Harbor in 1942, a German Me 262 and Me 163, and a completely restored Japanese A6M Zero.

However, it is the World War I aircraft exhibition that contains fantastic examples of original fighters. Of special interest is the Pfalz D.XII, a German fighter that entered service near the end of the Great War. A large number of Pfalz D.XII were built—approximately eight hundred. This was due to strong support from pilots who tested the type. During this testing, the Pfalz D.XII was considered comparable to the Fokker DVII. However, once ordered and put in use, the Fokker DVII quickly became far more popular than any of the Pfalz types.

The Pfalz had its pros and cons. The sturdy construction allowed for high speed dives with a degree of stability. It was perfect for attacking observation balloons, which were usually heavily defended by antiaircraft guns. But the type was prone to spins and could stall with little warning. Even maintenance crews were critical of the Pfalz and preferred the Fokker VII, because the Pfalz had a great deal of wire bracing, which simply meant more checkpoints and more time on the ground.

Pfalz Flugzeugwerke GmbH was the manufacturer of the Pfalz D.XIII, designed by Rudolph Gehringer to replace the obsolete Pfalz D.III. Today, there are no known surviving D.IIIs. However, two flying replicas were built for the 1966 film *The Blue Max*. One replica was built from scratch, while a second was converted from a de Havilland Tiger Moth airframe. Both replicas are said to be currently based in New Zealand. Prior to World War I, Pfalz Flugzeugwerke produced Morane-Saulnier monoplane designs under license. These aircraft entered military service as the Pfalz A- and E-series. In September 1916, Pfalz began producing the first of twenty Roland D.I and two hundred Roland D.II fighters.

The Australian War Memorial's Pfalz D.XII, which holds serial number 2600/18, was given to Australian authorities as part of the terms of the armistice. It began its journey as a used aircraft held in France after the war. It made its way to England via steamer across the English Channel, followed by the long cruise to Australia. The Australian War Memorial displayed the aircraft from the forties to the sixties, but it had been mislabeled, suggesting that it was an aircraft that had been shot down by the AFC 4th Squadron.

Although a great example to have in any museum, the Pfalz is generally believed to have had little contact with Australian pilots during the war. It mainly served on the western front in approximately ten German squadrons known as "Jastas."

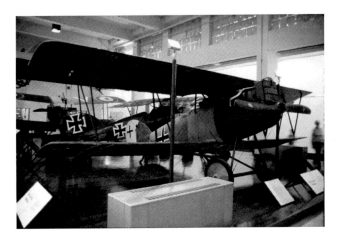

Pfalz D.XII—Australian War Memorial

Duigan Biplane

[Museum Victoria in Melbourne, Australia]

Dating back to 1854, the Museum Victoria in Melbourne, Australia, is an institution that today is made up of three museum venues: Melbourne Museum, the Immigration Museum, and Scienceworks.

Just a few miles from the center of Melbourne's business district, the museums represent a combination of the traditional static-artifact displays at one end of the spectrum and the Scienceworks facility, which features the very best of an interactive participation environment for the education of young visitors, at the other. Scienceworks also includes a planetarium.

With a collection as complete as that of Museum Victoria, it is not a surprise that Australia's oldest aircraft is found within it. The Duigan Biplane was built in Mia Mia, Victoria, in 1909 by John Duigan. Mia Mia is about seventy-five miles north of Melbourne and is a beautiful and spacious area known for its sheep farms and vineyards. Back in 1909, John Robertson Duigan made good use of the fields of Mia Mia, testing his flying machine. He built his aircraft from wood and metal and apparently utilized cloth treated with a rubber coating made by the Dunlop Rubber Company. The engine was a 25-horsepower four-cylinder design built by local J. E. Tilley.

Duigan's plane has the distinction of being the first aircraft built and designed in Australia to fly in the continent country. (Harry Houdini, the famed magician and escape artist, was the first person to fly in Australia—a story for another chapter.) The fascinating thing about John Duigan's aircraft is how it was designed. According to museum sources, the Duigan Biplane was built from Duigan's study of a postcard featuring a Wright Flyer. Using this, coupled with information from Sir Hiram Maxim's 1908 book *Artificial and Natural Flight* and various aviation journals, Duigan successfully built an airworthy craft despite never having been formally taught aerodynamics and never even having been in an airplane.

The Duigan Biplane flew most notably in January 1911. Duigan's audience numbered in the thousands, and the press took careful note of his achievements. Perhaps his motivation included an interest in winning a £5,000 prize offered by the Australian Department of Defense for an aircraft design that could be used for military purposes. As it turned out, the prize offer expired before Duigan could prove his plane's worth. Despite this, he remained undeterred and ultimately flew his plane at an altitude of one hundred feet for a distance of one kilometer.

In an attempt to make things official, John Duigan found his way to the Brooklands flight school in England and studied to receive his certificate. Using an A. V. Roe tractor biplane, he achieved certificate #211 in 1912. Once back in Australia, Duigan and his brother Reginald, who had always assisted him, came together again to build an Avro-like aeroplane that ended up crashing, resulting in major injuries to John. This setback would have been more than enough to deter further interest in the precarious sport of flying, but in Duigan's case, he courageously recovered and promptly joined the Australian Flying Corps in 1916.

As a lieutenant and the flight commander for No. 2 Squadron, he was sent to England. After being promoted to captain, he was sent in December 1917 to France, where he saw action with No. 3 Squadron (formerly No. 2 Squadron). At this point, flying an RE.8, Duigan fought it out with four German Jasta 6 Fokker Triplanes. John Duigan was awarded the Military Cross for gallantry due to this dogfight, which left him badly injured again. He was able to land his airplane and went about saving the life of his observer.

Today, a Duigan Biplane replica can be observed in flight on special occasions at the museum. Built in 1990 by Ronald Lewis, it was donated to the Victoria Museum in 2000 and now adds to yet another interactive aspect of this fine institution. In Mia Mia, there sits a monument that commemorates John Duigan as Australia's first homegrown aviator. And of course the original Duigan Biplane remains at the Victoria Museum, having been donated by John Duigan himself in 1920.

Sloane Biplane

[Yarrawonga-Mulawala Pioneer Museum in Mulawala NSW, Australia]

A bit off the beaten path, Mulawala in NSW, Australia, is where one will find a museum that possesses an old and very rare aircraft indeed. A less-than-complete but original biplane built by Douglass Sloane in 1913 is preserved among other unique pioneer Australian artifacts.

The museum describes itself as "especially rich in agricultural heritage, representing both wool and grain growing, as well as commercial and social life in the district. There is a large and diverse array of agricultural machinery with historical photographs of the equipment in use, and samples of wheat and other grains grown in the district." Yet despite such a description, early aviation enthusiasts will value a visit to lay eyes on one of Australia's oldest aircraft acquired by the museum. (It is unclear when it arrived.)

Other homegrown Australian aviation pioneers include Bert Hinkler and the aforementioned John Duigan, but Douglass Sloane was a tinkerer from Malwala Station who spent a great deal of time observing the flight of the wedge-tailed eagle. This interest in bird watching resulted in his own aircraft design. He built an engine and aeroplane and conducted experiments with great ambition in a science very new to the world. Ironically, it was this new science of aviation and Sloane's passion that would prematurely take his life in 1917. Douglass Sloane shipped off to England to fight in the Great War and died tragically in a flying accident. As reported by a comrade of Sloane's (No. 3 Squadron) and complied by author James Affleck, "The machine piloted by Lt Shapira and D (Tod) Sloane met with a mishap, which proved fatal. Engine trouble resulted in a nose dive, with a crash, which caused the loss of both lives of esteemed members of our Flight Squadron. Poor old Tod. The boys feel very sad about his death."

Having built the biplane in his family's woolshed, Douglass Sloan stored his home-built aeroplane in the same shed to be flown upon his return, a return that was never to come.

Australia has a rich aviation history, especially in the early days. With great open space for flight experiments and early involvement in Europe's wars, aircraft were a useful means of defense, exploration, and entertainment. This was best illustrated in 1910 when the first powered, controlled flight was made in Australia by the visiting magician Harry Houdini. This was a demonstration flight at a place called Digger's Rest, Victoria, in a Voisin biplane.

Houdini had the French Voisin built expressly for him for $5,000. He soloed it for the first time in Germany in 1909. Upon coming to Australia, Harry Houdini attempted for a month to fly first in Australia. But due to windy conditions and mechanical difficulties, he didn't accomplish the proposed flight of three miles until March 21, 1910. (Australian John Duigan was the first countryman to make a powered, sustained flight in Australia, just three months after Houdini.)

Houdini was recorded as saying, "When I went up for the first time, I thought for a minute that I was in a tree; then I knew I was flying. The funny thing was that as soon as I was aloft, all the tension and strain left me. As soon as I was up all my muscles relaxed, and I sat back, feeling a sense of ease. Freedom and exhilaration, that's what it is."

Interestingly, Harry Houdini, ever the showman, photographed his flight and thereby became the first aviator to have documented the event on moving film.

It was Houdini's intention to continue flying his Voisin after finishing his successful Australian tour. With this in mind, he warehoused his plane in England with a plan to use it for travel between venues when on show tours (magic performances), but apparently he was never known to have flown as a pilot again. His Voisin has never been seen again although various searches have been pursued over the years.

Blériot XI

[Museum of Applied Arts and Sciences in Sydney, Australia]

Louis Charles Joseph Blériot, who was born in 1872, was well known for his engineering abilities. Having already successfully built a company that manufactured headlamps for the first automobiles, Blériot became interested in aviation before the Wright brothers made their first flight. Starting with ornithopters (aircraft that attempt to fly by mechanically moving their wings) and moving quickly to glider experiments, he became friendly with Gabriel Voisin, who had already built and flown gliders. The two decided to go into business together, and the first of several Blériot aviation companies was established. This first company, called Ateliers d'Aviation Edouard Surcouf, Blériot, et Vois, conducted business in 1905 and 1906 but failed to create a powered aircraft. However, lightweight Antoinette engines developed by Léon Levavasseur eventually came to Blériot's attention and would provide the inspiration for a power source that could successfully lead him into the air.

As early as 1907, Blériot, who had by this point parted ways with Levavasseur to form his own company, designed and flew a monoplane that, although unstable and very dangerous, flew successfully utilizing a 50-horsepower V-16 Antoinette engine. The Blériot VI, as it was called, was one of many stepping-stones toward the construction of the Blériot XI, the plane that he used in 1909 to become world famous by making the first flight across the English Channel in a heavier-than-air aircraft. This feat won him the small prize of £1,000 offered by the *Daily Mail* newspaper and earned him a place in history.

Always an effective businessman, Louis Blériot purchased the Société Pour les Appareils Deperdussin, which was an aircraft manufacturer of which Blériot quickly became president. He renamed the company Société Pour l'Aviation et ses Dérivés or the more commonly used name, SPAD.

The Blériot XI became an iconic symbol of the early French aircraft, and the design was licensed out to other manufacturers or simply copied all over the world. In Australia the first airmail delivery was made in a Blériot XI in 1914 by stunt pilot Maurice Gauillaux. Gauillaux's Blériot XI exists today in the Powerhouse Museum, which is part of the Museum of Applied Arts and Sciences in Sydney, Australia.

It was this aircraft that Gauillaux used for loop-the-loop demonstrations for the joy of public consumption. Unfortunately, this was also the aircraft that Gauillaux was using in a demonstration flight that ended in a bad crash, leaving him in the hospital for six weeks. Once the Great War began, a recovered Gauillaux made his way to Europe, leaving his Blériot XI in Australia.

In 1916 the Blériot monoplane was sold to Robert Graham Carey from Ballarat, Victoria. Carey made this purchase to start a flight school in 1917. The school grew and eventually acquired several more aircraft for training purposes. One of Carey's students bought the Blériot XI from the school in 1920 and later offered it to the department of defense in 1937 for a small sum. By this time, however, the monoplane was in pieces and in poor condition. Almost discarded as trash while in storage, the Blériot was finally transferred to the museum, where it was kept and partially restored a few times before it was fully restored in 1981.

Along with the Sydney Observatory, the Powerhouse Museum makes up one of the two major branches of the Museum of Applied Arts and Sciences. The museum is essentially a vast and diverse collection of items of technology that includes everything from art to media to space technology. In existence in one form or other for 125 years, the museum contains more than four hundred thousand items. Along with early aircraft, some of the more interesting items include

- the Boulton and Watt steam engine, the oldest in the world, built in 1785;
- Locomotive No. 1, which was the first steam locomotive to carry passengers in New South Wales (1854); and
- the Strasburg Clock Model built in 1887, which is a working model of the famous Strasbourg astronomical clock in Strasbourg Cathedral.

Etrich-II Taube

[Technisches Museum in Vienna, Austria]

Founded in 1909 by Emperor Franz Joseph of Austria, the Technisches Museum Wien (Vienna) did not open its doors to the public until 1918. Having been delayed by World War I, the museum eventually housed collections of nature, astronomy, physics, mining, mass production, communication, information media, musical instruments, and transportation. Today, a visit to the museum is a worthwhile excursion for those interested in Austria's early aviation contribution. While Lloyd and Lohner are an important part of this history, the Technisches Museum has in its collection an original Aviatik and an Etrich Taube.

A close observer of the works of Otto Lilienthal, Igo Etrich focused his attention on early aerodynamics. His father, a business owner, had the means to assist Igo in his research and aided Igo in building the first of a few laboratories for the study of flight. Taking a slightly different approach to gliding than Lilienthal, Etrich studied the patterns of flight in descending seeds. Specifically, the seed Zanonia Macrocarpa assisted Etrich and his engineers, Franz Xaver Wels and Karl Illner (who later became the first Austrian to fly a glider in 1906) in developing their first glider called, not surprisingly, the *Zanonia*.

After years of experimentation, Etrich designed the Taube, which translates from German to "dove." (It also translates to "deaf person.") In 1910 the Etrich Taube flew for the first time. Subsequent flights, however, came with a high price, as the Taube crashed and severely injured Igo Etrich. Remaining enthusiastic about his design and with the assistance of his partner, Karl Illner, as pilot, Etrich refined the Taube for military use.

The Taube was considered a valuable commodity before the Great War and was purchased by the air forces of Italy and Austria-Hungary and the Royal Flying Corps in 1912. Prewar achievements in this type include the flight of Giulio Gavotti in 1911. It was Gavotti, an Italian aviator, who dropped the world's first aerial bomb from his Taube monoplane over the Ain Zara oasis in Libya.

Ultimately, Igo Etrich moved to Germany and founded the company that would eventually be called Hansa-Brandenburg; this occurred before the outbreak of war in 1914. Once hostilities began, Etrich felt obligated to allow all to copy his Taube design for the war cause. The Rumpler Taube quickly materialized, along with other, similar early fliers.

The Etrich-II at the Techniches Museum in Vienna was donated by Igo Etrich himself back in 1914. Built in 1910, it was one of fifty Etrich Taubes ultimately built, not including Lohner versions.

The Etrich Taube was viewed as the iconic early airplane. It had that ancient birdlike look, which is why the type was copied in the thirties for use in movies.

Alfred Friedrich, who was an early pioneer of aviation in Germany, founded a small aircraft factory after World War I. Friedrich was best known for long-distance flights that included a five-hour nonstop flight from Berlin to East Prussia. His company was established specifically to meet the demands of the exploding film industry, which needed realistic props for movies with a war theme. The Friedrich Etrich Taube is an aircraft built in 1936 to look and perform as if it were a 1913 Taube, with the landing gear being one of the most obvious modifications.

This particular 'early replica' can now be found in Krakow's famed aviation museum, where it is unrestored but interesting nonetheless. This aircraft, like others, was part of the German aircraft collection but moved to Poland once the bombing during World War II began.

Etrich-II Taube—Technisches Museum

Battaille Triplane

[Royal Museum of the Armed Forces and Military History in Brussels, Belgium]

The first organized air meet took place in France on a racetrack at a place called Betheny Plain, just outside the city of Reims. It only went on for a week in August 1909 but was an event that kicked off the air show industry that continues to this day.

The Reims show was a gathering of the world's best pilots and featured the world's various aircraft designs, all attempting to fly the farthest, highest, and fastest. Prizes in trophies and cash were aplenty. Reims and annual gatherings like it became the perfect promotional event for all who were to make a fortune at the 'dawn of aviation'.

It was perhaps the unique triplanes featured at Reims and another air show that same year at Tournai, France (Walther Bulot and Roe "tripes"), when Cesar Battaille was inspired to build his own three-winged aircraft. Battaille was an inventor with some wealth, as his father was the director of an industrial concern in Belgium. It was 1910 when Battaille began the construction of an aircraft of his own design. One of the first Belgian aviation pioneers, Battaille designed a triplane with a four-cylinder engine that allowed the craft to leave the ground in short hops only, and this was in 1911.

Of course, just three years later, the world turned to war, with Belgium being the flash point early on. Air meets were indefinitely on hold, and civilian-based aircraft design turned to the production of war-minded craft. Cesar Battaille was a member of the Belgian army as an architect of bombs. Specifically, he concentrated on bombs that could set ablaze the elusive zeppelins. It is a common misconception that zeppelins could be brought down easily, as they were filled with explosive gases. This was not the case. It took a great deal of ingenuity to develop bullets and other implements that could pierce the outer cover yet continue to burn until the hydrogen was compromised.

Once the war ended, Battaille seems to have given in to an interest in art rather than aviation. His triplane was hung in storage at his father's factory in the town of Basecles, Belgium. In 1971, the aircraft—or, more specifically, the remains of the triplane—were donated to the Royal Museum of the Armed Forces and Military History in Brussels. A restoration was undertaken by the Brussels Air Museum Restoration Society (BAMRS), and although much of the finished aircraft has been recreated, its base is as original and as old an aircraft as one can find. Included in the list of parts that had to be built from scratch were the fuselage covering, the upper fuselage itself, the seat, the steering wheel, a fuel tank, and a radiator. The original four-cylinder Grégoire engine was gone, but an appropriate replacement was chosen and installed. The Chenu engine chosen was from the 1908–1910 period and often an effective power plant for airships.

Because much of the restoration was undertaken from a study of photographs, the landing gear was created entirely by eyeing the images. Today, the triplane is posed gracefully on the first floor of the main hall at the museum and is a part of one of the best collections of World War I-era aircraft in the world.

Oftentimes referred to as simply the Brussels Museum, it enjoyed a very prosperous time just after World War I, thanks to the contributions of private families and foreign governments. With so many items and a strong focus on war material, a new location was founded at the Jubilee site. So it was in 1923 that the Military Museum was formally opened. Louis Leconte, a war veteran who had a source for obtaining abandoned

German war equipment, was made head curator. The museum was closed during the occupation years of World War II, but when it reopened to the public, many more subject sections were created. These include displays of science, old photos, and a military archive with a library.

Battaille Triplane—Royal Museum (Belgium)

Caudron G.3

[Royal Army Museum in Brussels, Belgium]

The Caudron Company was formed in 1909 by brothers Gaston and Rene Caudron. As was true for so many before them, fame came as result of their courage, viewed by ground spectators of their individual flights in and around 1910. A flight school followed, along with the attention of the French War Ministry. Just before World War I began, the Caudrons' school in Crotoy, France, hosted many of the first student pilots who would later fight in the war.

The Caudron G.3 was a highly effective reconnaissance and training aircraft in the First World War. Manufactured by the Caudron Airplane Company in France, the G.3 was particularly effective in mountainous terrain due to its ability to climb quickly. While flying the G.3 and representing the Caudron company, the French aviatrix Adrienne Bolland crossed the Andes mountains between Chile and Argentina in 1921, becoming the first woman to do so. As many as fourteen hundred G.3s were built in France, while still others were licensed to be built in Italy and England, accounting for another five hundred in service.

The G.3 had its engine up front within a nacelle but had a somewhat unusual tail spaced out from the fuselage, meeting at the back end. This gave it a very open look that was not conducive to fitted machine guns and other armament. However, at times small-caliber guns and bombs dropped by the pilot were in use. This lack of defense rendered this type obsolete rather quickly, and in 1916, the G.3 was pulled out of harm's way and used mainly for reconnaissance.

The Royal Army Museum's example in Brussels was built in 1923, later than most of the originals documented in this book, but it's a prime remaining example of a type that served so effectively over Europe and Mesopotamia. With the serial number 2351, this airplane spent much of its life in the hands of the Musée de l'Air et de l'Espace in Paris. This finest of institutions already had a Caudron G.3 so it was only fitting to arrange a trade, which ultimately resulted in the G.3 arriving in Brussels in 1975.

Records show that #2351 was used in the Caudron school into the thirties. From there, it was sold twice in France and was finally found in a barn and acquired by the Musée de l'Air in the fifties. Restored to airworthy condition by Jean Baptiste Salis, who is mentioned often in these pages, this artifact is now associated with the Memorial Flight Association at La Ferte Alais in Cerny, France. Salis formed Amicale Jean-Baptiste Salis (AJBS) in the early seventies to preserve and restore classic airplanes with the goal of keeping them flying. The website http://theaviationist.com reports, "Today, the association represents 300 members, of those about 60 are intensely active during the week and the weekend to keep some 30 historic aircraft flying."

Despite a strong air show resume in the late fifties, #2351 was retired in the midsixties, only to be enjoyed as a static display upon its arrival in Belgium. If the Musée de l'Air has the world's best collection of early original aircraft, then surely the Royal Army Museum in Brussels is not far behind. Well worth the visit while touring Europe, the Royal Army Museum boasts survivors in a very rare class. Such examples include Rumpler, Aviatik, Bataille, Zeppelin, Farman, Sopwith, and Schreck.

Kaspar Monoplane

[National Technical Museum in Prague, Czech Republic]

At the turn of the twentieth century, Europe was enjoying a period of stability, both politically and financially. Countries were looking to establish their own identities as well as to place high in a world order. However, unbeknownst to all, the century would start turbulently, with the world stumbling into a world war that few expected would end in a quagmire.

Prague, the capital city of the Czech Kingdom (as it was known before 1918), was a leader in technological development and decided to build an institution to dedicate and preserve information and artifacts related to these achievements. In 1908 this became a reality when the Technical Museum of the Czech Kingdom, today called the National Technical Museum, was established. The NTM was initially built up with the artifacts and possessions of earlier Czech collections, such as those of the Professional Engineering School, founded in the early 1700s, and the Czech Industrial Museum, founded in 1874. Early information contributors and participants in the new endeavor were not just university professors, but also Czech companies, Czech banks, and professional groups (unions).

After World War I, the Czech Kingdom became the Czechoslovakian Republic. The NTM acquired many of the finest examples of war aircraft in the world. However, the Second World War effectively closed the museum for many years. The museum reopened in 1948 in a limited capacity, with very little of its collection on exhibit. Specifically, the transportation gallery was established in 1950, but it was not fully accessible until 1990. When it was finally open to the public, the aviation treasures rediscovered were astonishing.

Although the full collection includes thirty-four aircraft, with some on exhibit at Kbely, the aircraft of greatest interest to us here include a Russian Anatra Anasalj, an American Morse LWF Scout, and an Austrian Knoller CII, among others.

One of the oldest aircraft in the Czech Republic, and perhaps the most famous, is the Kaspar Monoplane of 1911. Jan Kaspar, a graduate of Prague's Technical University, studied in Germany after college, where he had studied engines. Specifically, he concentrated on zeppelin airships and had a job at a factory that manufactured parts for airships. Kaspar, like so many aviation pioneers, was a natural mechanic, rode motorcycles, and raced cars.

Inspired by Louis Blériot's flights, Kaspar returned to his hometown in Czechoslovakia and attempted to create from scratch a monoplane of his own design. These apparently were dangerous flights and resulted in only marginal success in 1909.

Jan Kaspar made the decision to purchase a Blériot monoplane and make some modifications, mostly within the power plant. He removed the Anzani engine in the Blériot XI and switched it out with a Daimler water-cooled four-cylinder engine. This allowed for additional speed and the ability to cover a greater distance. Kaspar proved his modified Blériot was worthy of great recognition as he flew for the first time on April 16, 1910, thus becoming the first Czech pilot.

A year later, Kaspar built his own version of a monoplane very much like a Blériot. With this aircraft, called the JK, he flew from Pardubice to Prague in ninety-two minutes on May 13, 1911. The distance covered was seventy-five miles, with an average speed of fifty miles per hour. The twenty-eight-year-old Kaspar had become Czechoslovakia's first aviation hero.

Because of his fame and the notoriety of this airplane, Kaspar donated his Kaspar Monoplane to the National Technical Museum in 1913, where it has been all of these years. In 1966 it received a full restoration and was subsequently suspended by wires above the Transportation Hall, where it can be seen today.

Unfortunately, becoming an aviation hero and pioneer does not guarantee long-term success and happiness. Jan Kaspar, much like Alberto Santos-Dumont, committed suicide not even twenty years after his great flight. He suffered from mental illness and was financially impoverished.

Ellehammer Monoplane

[Danish Technical Museum in Helsingor, Denmark]

Born in Bakkebolle, south of Copenhagen, Denmark, Jacob Christian Ellehammer started his career as a watchmaker's apprentice. A tinkerer, he opened his own company in 1898. His company produced devices such as cigarette dispensers and soda machines. He progressed to experiments with combustion engines. Like Glenn Curtiss, Ellehammer was a successful motorcycle designer, and by 1904 his company produced its first cycle, called the Elleham. Concentrating on engines, he followed with an improved design of the first air-cooled radial design, which hosted three cylinders.

Completely unaware of the Wright brothers' flights in America, Ellehammer designed a flying machine that simulated the flight of birds he observed. He was quite successful in understanding the need for horsepower and put his new radial engine to use in his aircraft.

Jacob Ellehammer attempted flights with the underpowered engine he first designed. The power source was simply insufficient, so he built an 18-horsepower engine and attached it into a biplane. Looking like two kites on top of a tricycle, the aircraft's tractor propeller produced lift by filling the wings with air like a sail. Control was limited due to the absence of a rudder or fin, but the aircraft had a steerable tail wheel. There are many Ellehammer supporters who feel he should receive notice for being "first in the air," but as mentioned several times throughout these pages, to be an aviation legend, one had to achieve powered, sustained, *controlled* flight.

Despite this detail, in September of 1906 on the island of Lindholm, Jacob Ellenhammer became the first European to fly an airplane. This is the belief in Denmark and not necessarily internationally accepted. Most believe that Alberto Santos Dumont was the man who flew first in Europe, also in 1906. As it was, Ellehammer flew a couple of feet off the ground, for a little less than 140 feet. No matter what side you are on, this is a tremendous feat, considering the rabid interest in aviation by France and other European countries. In all, he made two hundred flights between 1906 and 1908.

Ellehammer quickly changed direction, however, this due to the advances made by so many others before 1910. His new interest focused on vertical flight, and in 1912 he succeeded in getting a craft off the ground. Vertical flight was still a long way from becoming efficient. This, coupled with the crash of one of his aeroplanes in 1916, led Ellehammer to resign his interest in aviation, but not before being indelibly linked with history (at least in Scandinavia) as one of the world's earliest powered-flight pioneers.

Ellehammer's accomplishments are honored in no small part in Helsingor, Denmark, at the Danish Technical Museum. Founded in 1911 the museum originally situated in Copenhagen contains an extensive aircraft collection, along with a display of everything from steam engines to bicycles.

The 1909 Ellehammer Monoplane Standard, as it was known, is part of the museum's collection, although it is not clear how much of it is original. This monoplane was the last of Ellehammer's aircraft designs. It has folding wings for ease of transport. In addition to the Ellehammer Monoplane and helicopter, in 2005 the Danish Technical Museum received from the Ellehammer family some of Jacob's personal items, documents, photographs, and movie footage.

Airco DH.9

Being a non-British member of the Imperial War Cabinet had its benefits. General Maharaja Sir Ganga Singh maintained this role during World War I. As the ruler of the Indian state of Bikaner from 1888 to 1943, Singh commanded the Bikaner Camel Corps (the animal, not the plane), which served in France, Egypt, and Palestine during the war. In turn, he received surplus aircraft as part of the Imperial Gift program.

The Imperial Gift was a program in which several countries representing the British Empire received surplus aircraft to build up their own air forces. Specifically, New Zealand, South Africa, India, and Canada received approximately one hundred planes each, as well as aircraft to replace any that were lent by these countries to England for the war effort. These were part of the twenty thousand estimated surplus aircraft available after World War I. General Singh received at least three Airco DH.9s for Bikaner. The Imperial Gift also included motorcycles, gear, transportable hangars in crates, support vehicles, and engines.

The DH.9s remained in storage in India for decades, with little knowledge of their existence among the rest of the world. In the late 1990s, this all changed when pictures of the DH.9s, taken by a man touring the Junagarh Fort, became available. Subsequent negotiations led by Guy Black's company, Historic Aircraft Collection LTD in England, resulted in the purchase and eventual preservation of two of the three DH.9s. One aircraft was already restored and part of a museum display in Bikaner, but the other two, although clearly valuable, were stored in an elephant stable at the time.

The DH.9 is a single-engine biplane that replaced the DH.4. It was designed as a strategic bomber and was built in large numbers. It was initially underpowered and started its war career in dubious fashion; ninety-four were scrapped or lost due to accidents. Another fifty-four were shot down. However, the DH.9 (the DH stands for de Havilland) was distinctly British and had some success with several pilots, including Lt. Arthur Rowe Spurling with five kills and Captain John Stevenson Stubbs with eleven victories. Although fewer than five DH.9s are preserved in countries outside of England, there was great interest in having this type preserved in fine institutions at home.

Today the featured aircraft, serial number D-5649 arrived at the Imperial War Museum (IWM) through a very productive set of circumstances in which one of Microsoft's founders, Paul Allen, purchased the IWM's Messerschmitt Me163 Komet Rocket Plane. This purchase provided the funds that allowed the IWM to purchase and restore the DH.9. This was clearly a win-win situation; the Imperial War Museum now has a more relevant and rare British plane as part of its collection, and Allen has added to his impressive collection, called the Flying Heritage Collection, based in Seattle, Washington, which is focused mostly on World War II.

D-5649 was built near the end of the war by the newly incorporated Alliance Airplane Company, part of Waring & Gillow Ltd, known for making furniture. It was Waring & Gillow that outfitted some of the interior of the *Lusitania*. Although it was to take part as a trainer for the 110th Squadron in Kelsey, United Kingdom, it is unlikely D-5649 ever saw duty. Records show it was slotted for storage, and from such a classification, it's easy to see how it ended up in India as part of the Imperial Gift.

Antoinette Type VII

[Science Museum in London, England]

Question: Who was the first to cross the English Channel in an aeroplane? If you said Louis Blériot, you are correct. If you said Hubert Latham, you were closer than you may know.

It was July 19, 1909, after several weather delays, when the first attempt to capture the *Daily Mail's* £1,000 prize for being the first to fly across the English Channel was undertaken, not by Louis Blériot but by the Antoinette-sponsored Hubert Latham.

Latham, who had toured the world from the Far East to the United States, was made of the same fabric so many other early aviators would become famous for. He was a confident and courageous risk-taker who viewed aviation as mankind's next great adventure. He had seen the Wright brothers fly in France in 1908 and knew what he wanted to do. After a search for a paying role as a pilot for a reputable and up-and-coming aeroplane company, Hubert Latham joined the ranks of the Antoinette Company. Antoinette was founded in 1906 by Frenchmen Jules Gastambibe and Leon Levavasseur to build engines designed by Levavasseur. Having already enjoyed a solid reputation for building boat engines, the Antoinette Company (named after Gastambibe's daughter) focused its attention on aircraft engines and, one year later, decided to build complete aircraft as well.

After some extensive training, Hubert Latham became a well-respected touring pilot for Antoinette. He spent a great deal of time on the road at aviation events, so it was only fitting that he attempt the channel crossing when the *Daily Mail* made their prize offer. Unfortunately, his initial record-breaking attempt would end in the water of the channel, after engine trouble came just eight miles into the flight. Unhurt, Latham planned to make another attempt that same month but was literally caught napping as Louis Blériot beat him into the air on the overcast night of July 25, 1909.

The worldwide fame Blériot achieved for the crossing eluded Latham, but he did continue to win prizes for his flying until his death in 1912 of suspicious causes. In 1911, Latham found himself on an expedition to seek out potential airfields in the French Congo. Officially, he died after being mauled by a wounded buffalo, despite his vast hunting and wildlife experience. Investigations revealed that his body was not mauled but had a single head wound that may have been caused by an intentional blow by one or more of his porters. The full truth may never be known.

The Antoinette Type VII was a redesigned and improved version of the Antoinette IV. It had increased engine power and utilized a wing-warping system developed by Levavasseur for the Antoinette V instead of the Antoinette IV's ailerons. Although beautiful and very much the ancient-looking "flying machine," very few Antoinette Monoplanes were built. The Antoinette Company ceased being an entity in 1912 and missed the demand for aircraft during World War I. Very few survive today, with notable exceptions in the London Science Museum, as well as examples in Paris and Krakow, Poland.

According to Leo Opdycke in his book *French Aeroplanes Before the Great War*, "The aircraft at the Science Museum in London, No. 50, is probably the most original (Antoinette); this No. VII was used by Latham and flown also by Robert Blackburn."

With an original fuselage and engine, the wings were skillfully constructed/restored by France's Jean-Baptiste Salis in 1958.

Antoinette Type VII—Science Museum

Cody V Biplane

[Science Museum in London, England]

Forepaugh's Circus was a travelling show in the United States in the late 1800s that featured all we've come to expect of a modern circus. These were the days when elephants were a rare sight, and Adam Forepaugh bred them to grow to be stars in his rings.

This early circus featured a Wild West show, in which "real" cowboys demonstrated their talents at horseback riding, lassoing, and especially shooting. And few were better at these activities than an Iowan named Samuel Franklin Cowdery, later known as S. F. Cody, who started performing with Forepaugh's in 1888 at the age of twenty-one.

Cody, who was born in Davenport, Iowa, just after the Civil War, was a natural showman. His exploits as a traveling cowboy are legendary, and he possessed true talent with a gun. As his interests expanded over the years, he had a knack for participating in whatever the latest craze was in Europe and in the United States at the time. In the early 1890s, he would race his horse against champion bicyclists; in the late 1890s, he experimented with Chinese-style kites. But as famous as S. F. Cody had become, his true calling was to blossom in England in the first decade of the twentieth century. Buffalo Bill Cody was a showman at around the same time and was often confused with S. F. Cody; they were not related, but each were famous in his own right.

While traveling in England with his Wild West show—his own company at this point—his experiments with box kites led him to realize the practical uses of his contraptions. Discussions with the British War Department about the feasibility of kites for observation purposes motivated Cody to further develop his kites. Eventually, they were to be used to do everything from carrying a man to pulling a boat across the English Channel.

S. F. Cody moved quickly to powered-flight experiments with the support of the war department, and on October 16, 1908, he made the first powered flight in Britain in his aircraft, called the British Army Aeroplane No. 1, using a 50-horsepower Antoinette engine he had purchased in France. He reached about eighteen feet, flew for about fourteen hundred feet, and was in the air for just thirty seconds. Clearly a courageous man, he flew over a set of trees and crash-landed after being hit by a gust of wind, which damaged Aeroplane No. 1. Later in 1909, Cody, who modified the aircraft extensively, flew for more than a mile, which at the time was the longest flight by an aviator in Britain.

In time, Cody earned the Royal Aero Club flight certificate No. 9, which is a bit ironic since he was the first to fly, not the ninth. He would go on to achieve a great deal as an aviator, including winning the Michelin Cup for the longest flight (again) in England in 1910, and he won a prize of £5,000 in the 1912 British Aeroplane Competition held on the Salibury Plain for his unique aircraft design.

The plane that he designed was called the Cody V, and two were purchased by the British military. Unfortunately, the first Cody V crashed, killing its pilot in January 1913. This resulted in an investigation of both the Cody Vs, and it was concluded that structurally they were unsound for various reasons, including wear and tear from testing.

The second Cody V, which was delivered to the British military in April 1913, was immediately retired and consequently donated that same year to the Science Museum in London where it is on display today.

Living a not-so-safe existence, S. F. Cody died on August 7, 1913, while testing a new design of his own called the Cody Floatplane. He and a passenger plunged out of the air from at least five hundred feet. It was clear how appreciated this American had become when an audience of a hundred thousand people attended his funeral. He was buried with full military honors at Aldershot Military Cemetery. It should be mentioned as well that S. F. Cody's only son died while flying for the Royal Flying Corps in 1917 during World War I.

Sopwith Pup

[RAF Museum in London, England]

The Royal Air Force Museum in the United Kingdom has locations at Cosford and Hendon and in the past had other locations as well—e.g., Saint Athan. The heart of the RAF collection can be seen in Hendon on the outskirts of London. It contains one of the finest aircraft collections in Europe, with particular excellence in the years of our specific interest.

Timed well for the hundredth anniversary of World War I, visitors can view one of the world's best-themed galleries, called "First World War in the Air," displayed within the Claude Grahame-White Hangar. This hangar is an original itself, as it was moved to the museum after having been built for use as part of Grahame-White's World War I aircraft factory. Claude Grahame-White was one of England's first pilots, having been trained in France at the Blériot school. He is probably best known for competing with French pilot Louis Paulhan in 1910 for the £10,000 prize offered by the *Daily Mail* newspaper for the first flight between London and Manchester to be completed in less than twenty-four hours. Even though the Frenchman actually won the prize, Grahame-White became a celebrity.

Hendon's World War I gallery features medals, uniforms, letters, and original aircraft. As the museum points out, "Eleven years after the first powered flight, aviation emerged as a force capable of changing the face of battle. In 1914, the Royal Flying Corps numbered just 1,500 people. By 1918, when the Royal Air Force was created, this had grown to more than 205,000."

Sopwith aircraft are fabulously represented at the RAF Museum, with originals of a Triplane, a Camel, a Pup, the remains of a Dolphin, and a partially original Snipe.

The Sopwith Pup, with serial number N5182, was built in 1916 by Sopwith Aviation Co. at Kingston upon Thames. Delivered out of Brooklands, which eventually became England's earliest and most prolific aircraft-manufacturing works (18,660 aircraft built in the twentieth century), the Pup saw action over Ostende in Belgium. According to operational logs obtained by the RAF Museum, it was over the sea near Ostende that this particular Pup scored only the second Sopwith Pup victory in the war. Although later damaged in further enemy contact, N5182 survived the war.

Ret. Lt. Commander Desmond Saint Cyrien discovered the remains of N5182 in the Musée de l'Air's vast reserve hold, which was a former airship hangar. This was in about 1959. According to the RAF Museum, it took Saint Cyrien approximately thirteen years and a bit of patient finagling to get the parts of the original Pup out of France and into England.

With a donation of original parts and instruments that had been missing, the Pup was fully restored, including an overhaul of the 80-horsepower Le Rhone rotary engine and a new propeller. The aircraft even received a Vickers gun from the Vickers Museum. For many years the Sopwith Pup was airworthy and participated in various events throughout the United Kingdom. It finally came to the RAF Museum in 1982 through a trade for a Spitfire with then-owner Doug Arnold. Sopwith Pup N5182 is considered 60 to 70 percent genuine and even comes with a letter written by Sir Thomas Sopwith himself attesting to its authenticity.

Bristol F.2B Fighter

[Shuttleworth Collection at Old Warden, England]

Airworthy survivors are in a class all their own. While there are several flying originals in Europe and the United States, the Shuttleworth Collection in Bedfordshire, England, at the Old Warden Aerodrome has far and away the best examples of airworthy authentic antiques. These include a 1912 Blackburn, a 1910 Deperdussin, a 1916 Sopwith Pup, a 1917 RAF SE5a, and the oldest flying original in the world, a 1909 Blériot XI. The Blériot XI at the Old Rhinebeck Aerodrome in New York is just three weeks newer than the Shuttleworth's example, based on manufacturer's date. Along with this menagerie of aircraft filling the skies, visitors can also view the Bristol F.2B, the subject of our discussion here.

So how did such a collection come about? As it turns out, the collection today can be credited in large part to Dorothy Shuttleworth, who established a trust in 1944, the Richard Ormonde Remembrance Trust, as tribute to her son, who died in 1940 while flying a Fairey. Dorothy also felt that such a cause would act as a platform to teach the science and practice of aviation. Richard, who founded the collection in 1928, was an automobile and aircraft enthusiast whose greatest interest was returning the old machines to working condition. Ironically, the Shuttleworth Collection was not viewable by the public until 1963, a surprise considering it is such a crowd pleaser today, with approximately twelve air shows per year. It should be noted that Old Warden Park is now also a conference venue and the location of the Swiss Garden and the English School of Falconry.

The Shuttleworth's Bristol F.2B Fighter with serial number D8096 was built in 1918 by the British & Colonial Aeroplane Company, Ltd., later to become known as Bristol. Delivered too late to see action in the Great War, it was used by No. 208 Squadron in Turkey in the early 1920s. D8096 was eventually sold in 1936 to Captain Christopher Ogilvie, who immediately stored it (possibly at Primrose Garages in Watford, UK, and/or a shed at the Elstee Aerodrome). The Bristol Fighter was deregistered on December 1, 1946. The Shuttleworth Collection acquired it and had it restored by the Bristol Aeroplane Company. It flew again for the first time in 1952. One of only two airworthy Bristol Fighters in the world today, D8096 was restored last in 1980.

It's important to remember that, at the start of World War I, Britain only had one hundred aircraft and only seven squadrons. The policy at the time was to purchase only aircraft designed by the Royal Aircraft Establishment. Pilots from the various squadrons had to lobby for their government to order the Bristol Scout. This pressure aided greatly in getting the Bristol Company recognized. This recognition led to further requests by the war department for specific-purpose aircraft.

The zeppelin threat was one of these highly regarded specific purposes, and the Bristol TTA was developed, followed by the Bristol F.2A, and in 1916, the highly regarded Bristol F.2B Fighter. The Bristol Fighter was so well liked that it was one of the most important British aircraft in the twenties. The F.2Bs were in service until 1931.

Although very much British, the Bristol Fighter was considered for production by the US Army Engineering folks. However, mistakes were made in choosing an engine for the American version, and an American-made Bristol Fighter never appeared in full production, although twenty-seven were ultimately built. The chosen American engine, the Liberty L-12, was a 400-horsepower behemoth simply too heavy, resulting in a nose imbalance unsuitable for effective flight.

After further design changes that included a wooden fuselage and a new engine choice (the Wright-Hispano engine), the American-built Bristol Fighter, known as the XB-1A, was built in small numbers. Specifically, three prototypes were built by the engineering division at McCook Field, and forty-four more were manufactured by the Dayton-Wright Company.

Bristol F.2B Fighter—Shuttleworth

Bréguet 14 A.2

[The Aviation Museum of Central Finland in Tikkakoski, Finland]

At the request of the French army's Section Technique de l'Aeronautique (S.T.Ae), four new aircraft types were to be proposed in different categories for production consideration. World War I was raging in 1916, and two of the categories, bomber and reconnaissance, needed vast improvement. The Bréguet 14, designed by Louis Bréguet and submitted to the S.T.Ae, served both functions. One hundred Bréguet 14A.2s were ordered to satisfy the reconnaissance requirement, and 150 Bréguet 14B.2 aircraft were built as bombers.

Louis Bréguet specialized in the design of aircraft that used a great deal more metal than those of other designers at the time. The Bréguet 14's fuselage was made of aluminum tubing for longerons and spacers. The main portion was constructed of welded steel tubes and braced with wire. The landing gear was mostly aluminum but braced with a steel channel. Despite the many steel parts found within the aircraft, the Bréguet 14 was lighter than wooden aircraft of the same size, and the metal allowed for a much more durable ship. Nearly eight thousand were built, having been in production long after the end of World War I.

As hostilities came to an end, it was decided that twenty French-built Bréguet 14s would be acquired by Finland. Originally, it was supposed to be thirty Bréguets, but the Finnish Aviation Forces felt that it would be more appropriate for there to be more seaplanes. With this in mind, twelve Georges Levy flying boats were added to the twenty Bréguets after the war. The Bréguets stayed in use in Finland until 1927.

The Finns were not the only ones to see the benefits of the Bréguet. The type was also purchased by the Belgian army and the United States Army Air Service, who bought more than six hundred aircraft. A good number of the Belgian and US Bréguets, perhaps half, did not receive the standard Renault 12 F engine, as it was in short supply. Instead, the Fiat A.12 was installed.

As in the case of the Finnish Bréguets, the type was used by other countries long after World War I. Specifically, they were used by the French while France occupied Germany. The French also used them in their colonies. Sources suggest that "a special version was developed for the harsh conditions encountered overseas, designated 14 TOE (Théatres des Operations Extérieures). These saw service in putting down uprisings in Syria and Morocco, in Vietnam and in France's attempted intervention in the Russian Civil War. The last trainer examples were not withdrawn from French military service until 1932."

Not a great deal is known about the original Bréguet 14A.2, viewable in the Aviation Museum of Central Finland (also known as the Finnish Air Force Museum) in Tikkakoski. It is serial number 3C30, a two-seat reconnaissance plane. It had a serial number of N1922 when in French use. It is known through photographs that 3C30 crashed sometime around 1925, resulting in broken wing parts. It is also known that modifications occurred through the early years, such as the addition of transparent windows in the floor of the rear cockpit.

Number 3C30 was restored by the Aviation Museum of Central Finland in 2000. It had apparently been in storage in a hangar in Vesivehmaa for decades, until it was rescued by the museum. This relic has the original oversize radiator and at one point had a second fuel tank hanging below that could be jettisoned. It also has a blue swastika, which invites a word here about the Finnish air force.

One of the world's oldest air forces, the Finnish air force was formed in March of 1918. Unlike many other air forces of other countries, the FAF was organized as an independent branch of the armed forces at the beginning. This allowed a unique opportunity to develop independent of other branches and therefore develop ahead of other air forces, both technologically and strategically.

The FAF received its first aircraft as a donation from a Swedish count named Erik von Rosen. It is because of von Rosen that we see the painted blue swastikas so prevalent on early Finnish airplanes. This was von Rosen's lucky charm, adopted by the Finns. These swastikas have no connection to the Nazi swastikas of the thirties and forties.

Avion III

The French entrepreneur Clement Ader shared his engineering genius in many ways but is remembered foremost for his aviation experiments. Born in Toulouse (where he also died in 1925), Ader specialized in electrical engineering. Credited with establishing an effective telephone system in Paris in 1880, Ader also created an apparatus much like today's stereo headphones. They were used on each ear and received different channels from live opera performances. This effectively eliminated the monotone effect a listener a great distance away would hear.

It wasn't long, however, before Ader caught the aviation bug. He began studying birds to understand aerodynamics. As early as 1886, he built his first flying machine called the *Eole*, named after the Greco-Roman wind god called Aeolos. This machine, looking more like a bat than a bird, was a steam-powered craft that may have lifted in the air for a very short distance. Powered, heavier-than-air flight in the 1880s was quite an achievement, but it took quite a few more years to achieve sustainable, controlled flight, which the Wright brothers are so famous for doing in 1903.

In any case, Ader sure cornered the market in building beautiful machines. His Avion III can be viewed today in the Paris museum, Arts et Métiers. The Avion III is/was another bat-like machine made of linen over wood. It has a forty-eight-foot wingspan and is powered by two propellers, each with four blades. Each of the two props was powered by a steam engine that produced twenty to thirty horsepower. Having been funded by the French War Office, Ader's Avion III may also have technically flown, but not to the satisfaction of the French army. Unimpressed with the future uses of Ader's experiment, the French stopped its funding. Despite this, Clement Ader's lifelong interest in aviation endured, and in 1909 he wrote a respected book on aviation called *L'Aviation Militaire* that accurately described the use and need of aircraft carriers.

Built between 1892 and 1897, Clement Ader's Avion III, sometimes called the Eole III, was not a successful aircraft and not one that was even copied. Few who saw it ever expected it to sustain manned flight. As the story goes, however, it seems the French kept Ader's attempts at flying in the Avion III a secret for many years. When the details surfaced, it was determined that the Avion III taxied a bit at Satory in testing, but with the great weight of two steam engines and elongated wings, a wind gust got the best of the craft and ended all of Ader's record-setting potential.

Contemporaries of Ader at this point in aviation's early development included Horatio Phillips, Otto Lilienthal, Lawrence Hargrave, Samuel Langley, and Hiram Maxim. The British Phillips, much like Hiram Maxim, built a steam-powered aircraft that was tethered to the center point of a circular space. His machine did leave the ground without a pilot and had no control. Hargrave and Lilienthal both focused on gliders and kites, which in hindsight did a great deal to improve the science of aeronautics. Samuel Langley probably gained the most interest in 1891, flying unmanned powered models. These successful models motivated not only Langley himself but also many others to solve the mystery of manned, powered, sustained, controllable flight.

Ader's Avion III was fully restored in the eighties and is perhaps the prize of the Musée des Arts et Métiers, outside of the original Blériot XI aircraft that crossed the

English Channel. According to Tom Crouch, the senior curator in the aeronautics department of the National Air and Space Museum, "Ader preserved Avion III in his workshop at Auteuil for several years. The aircraft was then displayed at the Paris Exposition Universelle in 1900, where it inspired Gabriel Voisin and other young aviation enthusiasts. The aircraft was then transferred to the Musée des Arts et Métiers in Paris. In 1906, upset by assertions that Alberto Santos-Dumont made the first public flight in Europe, Ader began to claim that he had flown at least 90 meters (300 feet) aboard Avion III on Oct. 14, 1897. Leading historians of flight soundly repudiated the claim but did not fully resolve the controversy."

To this day, many believe the French were the true pioneers of early aviation, despite the works of the Wright brothers.

Avion III—Musée des Arts et Métiers

REP 1

Man's relentless need for evolving technologically was never more evident than in the early days of aviation. A byproduct of this evolution and one of the more fascinating aspects of early aircraft design is the sheer artistic results. Pioneer French aircraft represent some of the greatest and most successful attempts at achieving flight. Early French aircraft perhaps represent the best of the notion of aircraft as art.

The Musée des Arts et Metiers (Museum of Arts and Crafts) in Paris is a converted abbey. The museum itself is a work of art, and its collections feature seven distinct segments that include scientific instruments, materials, energy, mechanics, construction, communication, and transportation. The objects are housed in the former church of Saint-Martin-des-Champs Priory.

Established in 1798, the museum holds some of the finest antiquities in the world. The museum has more than eighty thousand objects and fifteen thousand drawings in its collection, of which about twenty-five hundred are on display in Paris. The rest of the collection is preserved in a warehouse in Saint-Denis. An absolute must-see location for anyone with the slightest interest in viewing "firsts," as mentioned this shrine maintains the original English Channel–crossing Blériot XI of Louis Blériot, the creepy-looking masterpiece (that never flew) of Clement Ader, which is an 1897 steam-powered creation called the Avion III, and the first aircraft (that did fly) built of an enclosed steel fuselage, the REP 1.

Robert Esnault-Pelterie (REP) was a Paris-born scientist and inventor. Educated at the Sorbonne, he focused on chemistry, botany, physics, and later, engineering. Inspired by Wright gliders at the turn of the century, Esnault-Pelterie first experimented with his own gliders but quickly moved to powered flight. In 1907, he flew his REP Monoplane for the first time. Both engine and monoplane were completely of his design.

The REP 1 employed for the first time what we now refer to as a "joystick." The aircraft is a single-seater with a single wing (monoplane). It's designed in a tractor configuration (engine in front, pulled through the air) and powered by a 30-horsepower, seven-cylinder semiradial engine with a four-bladed propeller attached. The fuselage was built with steel, although the wings were constructed of wood covered with cloth (silk). Esnault-Pelterie placed a fixed fin and rudder under the fuselage and had a landing gear that consisted of just one wheel with an ingenious pneumatic shock absorber. A small wheel is found mounted on the rudder. Art meets functionality with unusual and strange-looking outer wheels fitted to the tips of the wings.

Made of steel tubing long before this construction technique was universally accepted, the REP was light and strong, traveling a distance of twenty-six hundred feet for its longest flight. However, in June 1908, with Esnault-Pelterie at the controls of another one of his monoplanes, a devastating crash left the pilot/inventor injured to the point that he'd never pilot an aircraft again. Injuries, reminiscent of Orville Wright's lifelong physical difficulties suffered after his crash with passenger Lt. Thomas Selfridge, plagued Esnault-Pelterie and left him unwilling to trust himself at the controls. Some sources suggest that the most serious injury was to his hands.

The scientist in him prevailed, however, and he made major developments in rocketry in the years after World War I. He believed that space travel was possible and likely most efficient using atomic power. To this day, Robert Esnault-Pelterie is credited with being one of the founding fathers of the Paris Air Show, the first all-aviation event when it started in 1909. Now biennial, it is also the most important aviation event in the world. Today, aircraft are controlled by a movable trailing edge of the wing, which is called the aileron. This method of steering an aircraft was developed by Esnault-Pelterie, a design more than one hundred years old but with little need for replacement.

Sopwith 1.5 Strutter 1 B2

[Memorial Flight at La Ferte-Alais, France]

South of Paris there is a special place called La Ferte Alais. It is here that Memorial Flight displays the organization's aircraft, most of which are from the World War I era. Since 1988, when Memorial Flight was established, it has concentrated on restoring and preserving aircraft to an exacting standard.

This includes all details from the original building techniques used to construct the originals to the materials and engine type used. This is important, as there have been many restorations that have been true to the original aircraft with the exception of its power plant, because the original engines often were underpowered and less efficient than, say, an engine that could be found and used yet had been built ten to fifteen years after World War I. The temptation to utilize an engine that is safer, lighter, and easier to find will always exist.

Memorial Flight has an arrangement with both the Musée de l'Air et de l'Espace in Paris and the Berlin Museum, while maintaining membership in the British Preservation Council. With such good company comes a network of rare parts, research, and technical data that otherwise would be impossible to acquire. Memorial Flight is a nonprofit organization that seeks to bring to the public the true thoughts and impressions of the players in the evolution of aviation in the early years.

A Sopwith 1.5 Strutter 1 B2 (serial number 2897) is part of the collection at La Ferte Alais and is the only flying original of this type in the world. Built in France, one of forty-five hundred with this distinction, not much is known about this particular aircraft's résumé. It has been concluded, however, that it is, in fact, a 1 B2, as there is an absence of metal wiring in the wings. Restoration began in 2001.

The 1.5 Strutter first appeared in the war late in 1915. It had a synchronized Vickers gun that shot through the propeller, which was a first for a British aeroplane. The observer was also well protected, as he had a machine gun mounted to the very effective Scarff ring. It's called a 1.5 Strutter because of the long and short pairs of cabane struts that support the upper wing. Cabane struts are simply the connectors between upper wings and lower wings and assist in transferring flight loads. These struts made of wood help maintain decalage (angle difference between the upper and lower wings of a biplane).

The Sopwith 1.5 Strutter was introduced after the period known as the Fokker Scourge, when German aviation proved to be formidable. The long range and aforementioned superior armament allowed the Sopwith 1.5 Strutter to be used for deep patrols into German territory with good success. However, its success as a fighter plane was short lived, as the lack of maneuverability of the 1.5 Strutter made it no match in dogfight scenarios with Germany's latest entry, the Albatros.

Ultimately, the 1.5 Strutter was used for reconnaissance, while the Sopwith Camel became the fighter of choice after its introduction in and around October 1917.

Santos-Dumont Demoiselle

[Museum of Air and Space in Paris, France]

Who flew first? Depending on who you ask and in what country you are asking, "The Wright brothers" is often not the answer. Whether it be Samuel Langley or even Gustave Whitehead, opinions vary greatly.

Alberto Santos-Dumont was born and raised in Brazil, and he died there, but he became famous for his aviation feats while living in France. The son of a rich coffee plantation owner, Santos-Dumont was an intelligent and technically skilled child. He loved the mechanics of steam engines and locomotives and purchased an automobile at the age of seventeen after moving to Paris with his family. A big fan of the works of the writer Jules Verne, Santos-Dumont studied chemistry, physics, and mechanics.

As early as 1900, Alberto Santos-Dumont was known the world over for his work with dirigibles. (The word *dirigible* is often associated with large rigid airships, but the term does not come from the word rigid but from the French verb *diriger*, "to steer.") He was perhaps best known early in his career for flying to and circling the Eiffel Tower in 1901, winning the Deutsch de la Meurthe prize. The award included 100,000 francs; Santos-Dumont promptly donated half to the poor of Paris.

With time Santos-Dumont turned to "heavier than air" flight and flew for the first time in October 1906, piloting the aircraft known as *14-bis* in front of a large crowd of witnesses. He flew for two hundred feet just three years after the Wright brothers flew at Kitty Hawk. The question that persists today remains what really constitutes sustained, controllable, unassisted flight. In Brazil, many believe the Wright brothers flew only because they were catapulted into the air with a weight and track system, and for this reason Santos-Dumont is the real hero of flight.

The Santos-Dumont Demoiselle of 1909, which came after the *14-bis*, was a completely different design, which is interesting, since so many inventors tend to improve on what they started with. The Demoiselle had a tricycle landing gear connected to a bamboo fuselage, with the pilot seated low and between the landing wheels. It employed a 24-horsepower Antoniette engine. The Demoiselle enjoyed a good deal of success and was copied by many.

Clément-Bayard, an automobile maker, decided that a mass-produced Demoiselle would be a profitable endeavor. The company switched the bamboo for steel tubes and priced that aircraft at 7,500 francs, a significant amount at the time but less expensive than other designs. In contrast to the actions of the Wright brothers, Santos-Dumont wanted to bring his design to the masses and refused to patent the concept. In fact, the drawings for the craft appeared in the American magazine *Popular Mechanics* in 1910.

As mentioned in these pages, the Musée de l'Air et de l'Espace is the finest aviation museum in the world for the period that this book covers. It is the oldest aviation museum in the world, and because it is located at Le Bourget Airport, it hosts the Paris Air Show every other year. It was started just after World War I, when Technical Chief of Aeronautics Albert Caquot recommended that a collection or conservatory of significant aircraft and aeronautical contributions be created. From this, the first pieces of different aviation collections were put together in warehouses in the suburbs of Paris, first at Issy-les Moulineaux in 1919 and then Chalais-Meudon.

While the original *14-bis* no longer exists, as its parts were used for later Santos-Dumont designs, it is no surprise that an original Santos-Dumont Demoiselle is found at the Musée de l'Air. The Demoiselle (meaning "dragonfly") in the Paris museum is a No. 21 type with a Darracq engine.

The story of Alberto Santos-Dumont doesn't end well. He last flew in a Demoiselle in 1910, just before becoming very ill with what turned out to be multiple sclerosis, which blurred his vision, preventing him from both flying and driving. This condition led to a deep depression that was to go on for two decades. Ultimately, Santos-Dumont returned to Brazil and committed suicide by hanging in 1932. People who knew him said that his illness was terrible for him, but they also reveal that he was plagued by guilt because of the ever-increasing use of aircraft in war.

Platform of Zeppelin LZ 113

[Museum of Air and Space in Paris, France]

Balloons, then airships, represented man's first experiences in the sky. The world's belief that man could fly was established with lighter-than-air machines. However, even after powered, controlled flight became a reality, lighter-than-air flying craft remained useful.

The zeppelins of World War I were rigid airships, also known as dirigibles, built in Germany from 1900 to as late as 1938. Zeppelins operated on the same principle as airships, utilizing interior bags that held hydrogen gas. However, zeppelins had a rigid structure, allowing for a more controllable and larger design. These large ships were the brain child of Count Ferdinand von Zeppelin, who was the founder of the Luftschiffbau Zeppelin Company. Civilian zeppelins were given names such *Graf* or *Hindenburg*, while military craft were given a designation of "LZ" during World War I, which in German means "Luftschiff Zeppelin."

The short history of the zeppelin, especially in the Great War, is fascinating and well documented in a myriad of volumes. But if one was to portray the zeppelin's true wartime effectiveness in just one word, that word would be "terror." By the end of World War I, zeppelins hadn't influenced the stalemate of the trenches but did greatly affect the strategy of defense for allied countries. English cities were terrorized by this silent menace that moved at first unnoticed at night with payloads of munitions simply dropped out of the sky.

Raids on England began in January 1915 with the goal of bombing Humberside (a port city), but high winds forced the two attacking zeppelins (L3 and L4) to drop their bombs on Yarmouth, Sheringham, and other surrounding villages. The results: four killed, sixteen injured, and minimal structure damage. This first attempt did leave all of England with the thought that even civilians were part of this war, and all could be reached by the "hand of the Hun." Ultimately, however, zeppelin activity revealed a weapon that was highly susceptible to ground fire, thereby costing the Germans many of the expensive craft.

Large bomber aircraft such as the Gotha were developed, and these proved more effective while also remaining effective tools of terror. Despite this Germany kept its zeppelins aloft with a last raid on England occurring as late as August 1918.

Zeppelin LZ 113, also known as L 71, which is the German navy designation, was a super zeppelin built at the end of World War I but one of a few that never saw action. Super zeppelins were built to attack enemy cities as far as five thousand miles away, such as New York.

Per the Treaty of Versailles, German weapons and aircraft were to be either destroyed or sent to various Allied countries for testing. In the case of LZ 113, the ship was sent to England, where it was scrapped without having been flown by an English crew. As it turns out, it's not easy to find a parking place for a zeppelin. This, combined with rapidly increasing technology, made the decision to demolish the ship an easy one.

Today preserved in excellent condition, the aft nacelle car of LZ 113 is on display at Paris's Musée de l'Air et de l'Espace at Le Bourget. The LZ 113 super zeppelin's first flight was on February 22, 1917. Although today suspended, one can take a staircase up to view the interior at eye level within the museum. This view reveals the cramped space where crew members would have performed their duties at great altitude in freezing conditions. This nacelle car (platform) contains three Mayback-type HS engines.

In the end the zeppelin concept turned out to be mostly ineffective as the war was coming to an end, but it was a concept that was proven to be at least feasible. In 1917, Germany built the L59, which was a lengthened super zeppelin modified specifically for long-distance flights. In November of that year, it began a flight toward East Africa. A distance of four thousand miles was covered, with the L59 flying nonstop for ninety-five hours, thus revealing itself a secret weapon capable of crossing the Atlantic. However, the fragility of the hydrogen-filled zeppelins once again reared its ugly head. In April 1918, L59 was sent on a mission to bomb the British naval base at Malta. It caught fire over the Straits of Otranto, and all crew members were lost.

Grade Monoplane

Often as historically interesting as the aircraft themselves, the museums that house these antiquities could have volumes written about them. One such institution is found in Munich and known most commonly as the Deutsches Museum.

With more than twenty-eight thousand items on display, covering fifty separate fields of science, the Deutsches was founded in 1903. Composed of a gorgeous set of buildings on its own island, the museum possesses branches in Munich and Bonn. Of most interest to aviation enthusiasts is the Flugwerft Schleibheim branch, located eleven miles north of the center of Munich. The airfield and its historic buildings were built between 1912 and 1919 by the Royal Bavarian Flying Corps.

In Schleibheim, a visitor can see an original Fokker DVII and a Vollmoeller monoplane from 1910. However, found not in the aviation-specific Deutsches at Schleibheim but in the main location in Munich is the subject of our discussion, an original Grade monoplane. It is one of only two in the world, with the other one displayed in the Technical Museum in Magdeburg, Germany.

Hans Grade is best known for being the first German to fly over German soil, which he did in a triplane that he designed; establishing Germany's first flight school; and designing the monoplane that was first to deliver mail via the air in Germany.

His Grade monoplane, now in the Deutsches, is configured with the pilot sitting below the wing. The aircraft uses a cabane (a framework supporting the wings at the fuselage) for the pilot to sit in. It is covered in fabric, while the forward struts support the main landing wheels. Most unique is the single boom that acts as the main structure from which stability is achieved. The steering comes from wing warping, and the engine is an 18-horsepower two-stroke engine built by Grade himself. With an aluminum propeller, this monoplane is similar in appearance to a modern ultralight.

The monoplane was first flown in 1909, and it wasn't long before Hans Grade entered competitions and won prizes for aviation achievements. This included the Lanz Prize, won by flying in a figure eight for a distance of two kilometers. The Grade Monoplane also won events for speed and distance in Egypt at the Helipolis aviation meeting in 1910. One of Grade's monoplanes was purchased by the Japanese army and subsequently became the first aeroplane to be flown in Japan.

The Deutsches Museum acquired the Grade Monoplane in 1917. Also referred to as the "Libelle" (dragonfly), the Grade Monoplanes were built from 1909 to 1914. Approximately eighty were built with a relatively low price of 12,000 marks, which included flight training. The Deutsches example was the first powered aircraft acquired by the museum. The original engine also exists today and has been removed and is displayed separately; both can be found in the Old Aeronautics Hall.

Ultimately, Grade decided that establishing an automobile company would be more lucrative than aircraft construction after World War I and founded Grade Automobilwerke AG. In a rather nostalgic gesture while celebrating his sixtieth birthday, Hans Grade flew his original monoplane once again. He flew for eighteen hundred feet at Berlin Tempelhof Airport, quite an accomplishment for a fragile old machine (the airplane, not the man).

Wright Standard Type A

[German Museum of Achievement in Science and Technology in Munich, Germany]

Orville and Wilbur Wright were inseparable brothers and the sons of a bishop of the United Brethren in Christ Church. Wilbur, the older and more conservative of the two, felt that there was enough information on aerodynamics to warrant an investigation into building a workable flying machine that could achieve heavier-than-air, sustained, controllable, powered flight. These four attributes were essential, as controlled gliders had already proved effective. Early on, the weight and design of an engine was the main issue. Later, full control of the aircraft through wing warping had to be honed.

The Wright brothers conducted many of their experiments on Huffman Prairie outside their home town of Dayton, Ohio. Kitty Hawk, North Carolina, is most often mentioned in history books as the place where the Wrights became skilled at flying; Huffman Prairie may better deserve this title. However, Kill Devil Hills at Kitty Hawk did provide the brothers with the best environment to experiment with glide technique. The wind and flat landing terrain were perfect, to say nothing of the privacy the Wrights so often sought.

The Wright brothers were very protective of their invention. Proved to work on December 17, 1903, the Wrights did their best to hide their achievement from the public. So concerned with the possible copy or theft of their idea, they took steps to disappear from the years from 1903 to 1908, until a patent was finally granted. These years were used to perfect the airplane, but by this time, many others all over the world had their own versions of a powered flying machine.

The Wrights shrewdly took it upon themselves to arrange a European tour to emphasize flight demonstrations with a goal of conducting negotiations to manufacture Wright airplanes for those organizations and countries that were interested. The United States had interests in the Wrights' invention but were slow to draw up contracts and make significant purchases.

One of the greatest successes of the Wrights' European travels was the destruction of the notion that the Wright aircraft was overrated and not as effective in the air as competitors' machines. In fact, the European audiences were flabbergasted by what they saw. The Wright demonstrations featured the Wright Model A, which was similar to the 1905 Wright flyer. Two hundred flights were made over a one-year period in Europe.

Despite the fact that so many licensed Wright aircraft were built in Germany, the original Wright Model A found in the Deutsches Museum in Munich is the only remaining Model A built in Dayton, Ohio. It was the aircraft used for demonstrations in Germany in August 1909. The museum received this rare plane only to see it damaged in World War II. In 1958, it was restored for public viewing.

As most schoolchildren know today, the Wrights started their transportation empire by designing and manufacturing bicycles. Very few actual Wright bicycles exist today, and all can be found in the United States. There are five known to exist. There are two at the Carillon Historical Park in Dayton, Ohio, hometown of the Wrights. Two are owned by the Henry Ford Museum, one of which is on loan to the Smithsonian National Air and Space Museum. And there is an original Wright bicycle at the National Museum of the US Air Force in Dayton, Ohio.

Ansaldo A.1 Balilla

[Museo del Risorgimento di Bergamo in Bergamo, Italy]

Long before its aviation initiatives, Ansaldo was a highly respected engineering company in Italy that remained in business for 140 years (1853–1993). Beginning with railroad projects and expanding into the shipbuilding industry, Ansaldo was well established in both capital and political positioning for weapons manufacturing just as World War I was beginning. By the end of the war, Ansaldo employed eighty thousand workers.

The Ansaldo A.1, called Balilla after an Italian folk hero, was the only Italian fighter aircraft manufactured in Italy during World War I. Another Ansaldo design, the SVA.5, was originally conceived to be a fighter but was ineffective in this role; it thereafter proved its worthiness as a reconnaissance airplane instead. The A.1 was basically a redesign of the SVA.5, but due to its newly intended fighter role, it had a larger engine and other modifications. One interesting revision was the inclusion of a hatch that allowed the fuel tank to be jettisoned if an onboard fire occurred.

The A.1 joined the fray just four months before the armistice, but due to a lack of maneuverability and the general difficulty to fly, the A.1s remained close to home as defensive weapons. Despite this, the Ansaldo was fast and did score one victory before the war ended by downing an Austrian reconnaissance plane.

Perhaps the Ansaldo A.1's greatest contribution was its role in helping the aviation industry capture the attention of Italians. The A.1s were used to promote Italian aviation and were seen frequently in flying demonstrations across the country. Most of the publicity was garnered by Italian aviator Antonio Locatelli, a decorated pilot who flew with the famous Gabriele d'Annunzio's air squadron. Postwar celebrations were frequent with Locatelli in attendance, but it should be remembered that he had engine trouble with his new aircraft during the war and was forced to land behind enemy lines, where he was held captive for a short time.

It is in honor of Locatelli that an Ansaldo A.1 from a batch of 150 built in 1917 was given to the city of Bergamo (birthplace of Locatelli) in the twenties. This is the aircraft (serial number 16553) that now resides at the Museo del Risorgimento di Bergamo. The Turin chapter of the Italian the aircraft restoration society Gruppo Amici Velivoli Storici (GAVS) restored the A.1 to its original glory. Rescued in 2000 from the second floor of the Bergamo medieval castle, where it had been placed long before, the aircraft underwent a restoration process consisting of six thousand hours of work and resulting in a static original World War I aircraft with incredible detail.

The painting on the side of the craft is "Saint George Killing the Dragon" and was preserved as much as possible. Fabric from the wings had to be discarded, as it had deteriorated. The original Vickers machine gun was reinstalled, having been removed and exhibited alone in another part of the museum.

GAVS did such a fine job restoring the engine (a 220-horsepower SPA 6A) that it is exhibited on its own next to the A.1 to illustrate its detailing. In the aircraft itself, there is a mockup of the engine with the propeller in the correct position.

Ansaldo A.1 Balilla—Bergamo

SPAD S.VII

[Museum of the History of Italian Military Aviation in Vigna di Valle, Italy]

Italy, much like France, has an extremely rich history in aviation, especially in the earliest years. Effectively, this history began in 1909 when Wilbur Wright was invited to Rome, where he trained Lieutenant Savoia of the Italian army and Lieutenant Calderara of the Italian navy. It was Mario Calderara who was credited with being the first Italian pilot to solo.

Italian museums have done a good job of preserving their early aviation artifacts. There are many early originals found in Italy, with many noteworthy individual examples including several Caproni, Ansaldo, and Macchi survivors.

The Museum of the History of Italian Military Aviation (or the Italian AF Museum for short) is located in the town of Vigna di Valle on Italy's Lake Bracciano. Appropriately, this is where the earliest aviation experiments were conducted in Italy as far back as 1904.

The AF Museum is designed to highlight Italy's aviation history. The museum houses forty-two thousand square feet of exhibit space divided into four large hangars, used to display more than sixty aircraft and a vast collection of engines, artifacts, and documents. The hangars represent chronological stages of aviation history including the First World War, represented superbly in the Troster Hall.

Troster is the oldest aeronautical building in Italy and contains nearly four thousand square feet of exhibition space housing the oldest aircraft in the collection. The building itself is a World War I survivor, having been built around 1915. It was given to Italy by Austria as part of war reparations. Within this hall the early aviation enthusiast can gaze upon one of only two Caproni bombers in the world. Also on display is an Ansaldo SVA, an ancient military balloon from 1804, a Blériot SIT (a rare two-seater) that was used in Italy's war with Libya during the twelve months of 1911–1912, and two noteworthy SPADs.

Both of the SPADs are original S.VIIs. One of the SPADs belonged to Ace Fulco Ruffo di Calabria, who achieved twenty victories during World War I. His aircraft "S-153" (more accurately, with serial number S.1353) is the oldest SPAD in the world, having been built in 1916. The other SPAD belonged to Ace Ernesto Cabruna.

Fulco Ruffo di Calabria, known for his distinctive black skull-and-crossbones emblem on the side of his airplanes, served quite effectively for the budding Italian air force during the Great War. He began not as a fighter pilot but as a member of a two-seater artillery coordination squadron known as the 44a Squadriglia Artiglia. He received two bronze medals for military valor in this role in 1916. After some extensive training on Nieuports, Ruffo was moved to the 1a Squadriglia as a fighter pilot. Alongside Ruffo in many a battle was perhaps Italy's most famous World War I fighter pilot, Francesco Baracca. Baracca had on his plane the prancing horse insignia that was later borrowed by Enzo Ferrari as his car company's logo. Ruffo and Baracca scored kills on missions together more than once.

SPAD S-153 was a gift given to Ruffo after the war by the Italian government in honor of his service and his twenty victories. The SPAD S.VII spent many years travelling as an exhibit representing Italy's military aviation prowess. Ruffo donated the aircraft back to Italy by way of the air force academy in the thirties. It was thoroughly restored by Gruppo Amici Velivoli Storici (GAVS) in Rome in 2001 and can now be viewed with its original insignia and color scheme at the AF Museum. During this restoration, it was discovered the construction date was 1916, proving S.153 to be the oldest SPAD in the world.

Rumpler Taube

[Norwegian Armed Forces Aircraft Collection in Gardermoen, Norway]

Norway's aviation beginnings were a bit behind other European nations, having the first recorded flight coming as late as 1912. Although attempts to fly came in 1910 by Einar Lilloe Gran, they were apparently unsuccessful. Hans Dons on June 1, 1912, made the first sustained powered flight in Norway by a Norwegian pilot flying from Horton to Ora near Fredrikstad. He accomplished this feat flying the HNoMS *Start*, a Rumpler Taube carefully preserved today in the Norwegian Armed Forces Aircraft Collection in Gardermoen.

The Rumpler Taube was a German aircraft first built in 1909. "Taube," which is German for pigeon or dove, was designed by Igo Etrich and manufactured under license by Rumpler. Although there were many variations of the Taube by different companies such as Gotha, Albatros, and Halberstadt, the aircraft types were so similar that many were nearly indistinguishable to the naked eye. The Taube consisted typically of a two-seat configuration made of wood and covered in canvas. The engine varied but was usually a four-cylinder Argus or a six-cylinder Mercedes. The Taube was essentially designed to be a two-seat reconnaissance aircraft, and that is how it was used at the beginning of World War I.

A Taube was used before the war, however, in 1911 when the Italians engaged the Turks in Libya. A hand pistol was used as well as small bombs dropped in the raid. Once World War I began, the Taube was used extensively simply because there were so many that made up Germany's early air force. But the Taubes saw little action after the first six months, as more sophisticated war aircraft were designed, built, and brought to the front.

Though a short stint in World War I, the Taube did see action in China of all places, as Germany had stationed two Taubes at Qingdao. A Rumpler Taube piloted by Lt. Gunther Pluschow was tasked with attacking a Japanese contingent of eight or more aircraft and several navy vessels. Pluschow did little damage to the Japanese force but is now remembered for flying top-secret documents to Shanghai, which he accomplished just before Quingdao was overrun by the Japanese.

The Norwegian Armed Forces Aircraft Collection's Rumpler Taube, called *Start*, was built as a floatplane and purchased in Germany by the Royal Norwegian Navy. It therefore became Norway's first military aircraft. It was purchased with funds from private sources as well as known contributors such as King Haakon VII of Norway, who was the first king of Norway after 1905, when Sweden and Norway were no longer united. It was the courageous Haakon who years later, as an elected monarch, united the Norwegian people after the Nazi invasion.

Rumpler Taube *Start* was ultimately gifted to the Norwegian navy not long after its first successful flights in 1912.

Rumpler Taube—Gardermoen

Sopwith Camel

[Polish Aviation Museum in Krakow, Poland]

One of the oldest aerodromes in the world is found in Krakow, Poland. Most recently called the Krakow-Rakowice-Czyzyny Airport, it was established in 1912 by Austria-Hungary. It was closed to all major air traffic in 1963 except for police helicopters and an occasional fixed-wing aircraft, but its runway is also used as a rather convenient method of ferrying some of the collection or acquired new exhibits of the Polish Aviation Museum. This museum opened at the airport just after normal operations ceased in the midsixties. It is considered one of the best aviation museums in the world with an incredible collection of originals specific to our particular interests (1903–1920). Within its halls are found six survivors, all of them the only remaining examples of their types left on earth. They include an Aviatik C.III, a DFW C.V, a Geest Mowe IV Monoplane, a Grigorovich M-15, an LFG Roland D.VI, and an LVG B.II.

And what would an award-winning collection be without an original Sopwith Camel? The Polish Aviation Museum has a Lincoln-built (England, not Nebraska) example in its possession. With serial number B7280, this Clayton & Shuttleworth factory example was shot down in Belgium behind German lines in September 1918. The pilot, Captain Herbert Patey, was taken prisoner.

At the time, Patey had eleven kills and had been awarded the Distinguished Flying Cross just two days earlier. A victim of Ludwig Beckmann of Jasta 56, Patey survived his imprisonment only to die a premature death in the influenza epidemic that ravaged the world just after World War I.

B7280 had little damage and was repaired and flown by the Germans before ending up in the aeronautical exhibition in Berlin. During World War II, the Camel was moved along with several other important aircraft to Poland to avoid the routine bombing of Berlin. Sopwith Camel B7280 is likely the most interesting surviving Camel in the world today due to its war record. Altogether, eleven German aircraft were shot down by this Camel's guns, nine aircraft by Captain Patey flying for the 210th Squadron, and two others shot down by J. H. Foreman prior to moving to the 210th.

Let's remember that the Sopwith Camel was notoriously difficult to fly due to the spinning effect from the Clerget rotary engine, plus the weight of the aircraft's front half, which saw 90 percent of the Camel's total weight in the front seven feet. This allowed for excellent maneuverability but considerable lack of stability in flight. In any case, the Sopwith Pup and Sopwith Triplane, two relatively simple airplanes to fly, were out of use, replaced with the Camel, which was built in large numbers; nearly fifty-five hundred were produced. The Camel was employed to a great extent as home defense but did enjoy dogfighting success most notably with Major William Barker, who had the most victories in RAF history with forty-six.

The Camel served first for the Royal Naval Air Service in June 1917 in and around Dunkirk, France, with No. 4 Squadron. Soon after, No. 70 squadron of the Royal Flying Corps. had Camels and by 1918, thirteen squadrons with flying Camels. When the Germans began their nighttime Gotha bombing campaigns of British cities in 1917, the Sopwith Camels proved effective in the dark. They were fitted with navigation lights and had their Vickers guns replaced with over-the-wing Lewis guns.

Not long after the Camels proved that they were not so blind in darkness, they were used at night to attack German airfields. But as with all war technology developed so fast, the Camel's relatively slow speed and low ceiling led to decreased use as soon as the middle of 1918. It was not taken out of service altogether, however, because of the late start of its replacement, the Sopwith Snipe.

Schreck FBA Type B

Established in 1913, Franco-British Aviation, best known by its initials (FBA), was a London-based aircraft manufacturer founded by Louis Schreck and Andre Beaumont that produced aircraft in France. Timed well for the start of the Great War, FBA produced seafaring aircraft for the French, Italian, Russian, and British war efforts.

Like the Farman brothers and other aviation pioneers of the time, Louis Schreck sold automobiles at first. A Frenchman, Schreck learned to speak English and Spanish while traveling selling cars in North America in the early days. This is also when he learned of the Wright brothers. It didn't take him long to leave the auto business and start anew in aviation. He was twenty-eight years old in 1908 when he purchased a Wright biplane to fly back in his home country.

Once the war had begun, Schreck FBA produced its first success, the Schreck FBA Type A. Manufactured in good numbers, with 125 going to the English and far smaller numbers (between ten and twenty each) going to Russia, Denmark, and Italy, Shreck FBA was a viable business. Late in 1914, a two-seat version of the Type A with a reinforced hull and the ability to fold its wings for transport and storage was created. Called the Schreck FBA Type B, it was built in good numbers as well, with some 150 manufactured.

Finally, in 1916 a Type C was built, which essentially was a Type B with a larger engine: a Clerget 9B 160 horsepower. Three hundred C Types were built at a point when other manufacturers took notice of the world's need for seaplanes. Competition from Donnet-Leveque, Tellier, and Levy Besson resulted in financial issues for Schreck, even though he did win major orders for the Schreck Type H. At the end of World War I, the need for submarine-seeking bombers and reconnaissance seaplanes had quickly ended, and so had the Schreck FBA successes. Louis Schreck's company closed, but not before he won the Cross of the Legion of Honour for his war contributions. His company closing did, however, make him a wealthy man.

In Portugal two FBA Flying Boats of the B Type were placed on the Tagus River not far from Lisbon for the purpose of training the first Portuguese military pilots. By September 1917, these aircraft would make up part of the Centro de Aviacao Maritima, which was the first Portuguese naval air station.

The Museu de Marinha in the Belem section of Lisbon, Portugal, features, as one would expect, some of the finest examples of seafaring antiquities in the world. As the museum points out, "The museum's rooms provide a reflection on the connection between Portugal and the sea, the Portuguese discoveries and their impact on the formation of the modern world." What may be a surprise, however, is this marine museum also maintains an exhibit of two early aircraft, a Fairey D and the Schreck FBA Type B. Both are exquisitely original and, in the case of the Schreck, painstakingly restored in 1999.

This Schreck FBA Type B, known as the n.2, is the oldest aircraft in Portugal. It was discovered that it is a combination of two Schreck FBAs with the fuselage from an n.2 and the wings coming from an n.1. The FBA has the original engine, a Gnome monosoupape that had been cut away at one point, most likely for training students.

The Fairey D in the museum holds a special place in Portuguese history because it is a record setter and the sole surviving Fairey D. The aircraft, No. 17 serial F.402, named *Santa Cruz*, was involved in a transatlantic crossing attempt by Portugal in 1922. For the crossing, the crew used a modified Fairey IIID named the *Lusitânia*, which had its wings and landing gear altered for the long journey. Once underway in March, the Fairey III crashed at the S. Pedro Rocks off the Brazilian coast while attempting to land to refuel. The crew completed the journey with a standard Fairey III D (No. 17 serial F.402), which landed in Rio de Janeiro on June 17, 1922.

Sopwith Triplane

[The Central Museum of the Air Forces in Monino, Russia]

Sopwith, also referred to as Sopwith Aviation Company, Kingston on Thames, was a British manufacturer. Original Sopwith aircraft are a rare possession for any organization and precisely why seeing one in Russia may be a bit unexpected. Even harder to find are original early triplanes. After all, there are no surviving Fokker triplanes (Dr.1), the cultural icon flown by the Red Baron.

There are only two original Sopwith Triplanes left in the world. Despite this, the Central Museum of the Air Forces in Monino, Russia, is the proud owner of one of these unique examples. The other is found in the RAF Museum in the United Kingdom, with serial number N5912. (Note: There is a fine reproduction Sopwith Triplane flying at England's Shuttleworth Collection. It is so keenly accurate that Thomas Sopwith himself referred to it as "a late production" example.)

The Sopwith Triplane was an experiment for the Sopwith Aviation Company. Its development was not initially paid for by the government as it was an internal Sopwith project that was based mainly on the Sopwith Pup. Designed by Herbert Smith, the Tripe, as it was called, had three wings that among other things allowed for a better view for its pilots, an important characteristic in 1916, as dogfighting was common at this point. The Royal Naval Air Service was given the aircraft to test, and the Sopwith Triplane was successful. It was agile and highly maneuverable, much like other triplane designs.

Once ordered for production, the Sopwith Triplanes were given the 130-horsepower Clerget 9B rotary engine. Contracts consisted of relatively small numbers: ninety-five aircraft to be built by Sopwith, forty-six to be built by Clayton & Shuttleworth Ltd., and another twenty-five aircraft to be manufactured by Oakley & Co. However, development of more advanced aircraft types was coming up so fast in 1917 that the contracts for the Sopwith Triplane were either transferred or canceled. The triplane became obsolete very quickly, and the Sopwith Tripe was effectively replaced by the SPAD S.VII and the Sopwith Camel. Only 147 Sopwith Triplanes were built in total, and only three were built by Oakley & Smith before the contract was dissolved.

Although brief, the Sopwith Triplane enjoyed some notable success. The No. 10 Naval Squadron, consisting of all Canadian pilots and known as the "Black Flight," succeeded in scoring eighty-seven air victories in just three months. Led by Raymond Collishaw, who himself shot down thirty-four German aircraft in the Tripe, members of the Black Flight could be recognized by their black cowls. Much like Richtofen's Flying Circus, Colishaw's Black Flight had names for individual aircraft such as Black Maria, Black Prince, Black George, Black Death, and Black Sheep. Colishaw ultimately scored sixty total victories in various aircraft types.

The Central Museum of the Air Forces at Monino, which is some thirty miles from downtown Moscow, was once called The Russian Federation Air Force Museum and, prior to that, The USSR Air Force Museum. From the early 1930s to 1956, it was an active Russian air force base. The museum opened in 1958 after airbase activities ceased. Today, some sources report that non-Russian tourists may need permission in advance of a visit. The Sopwith Triplane now in Monino and likely having serial number N5486 found its way to Russia in 1917 for testing and evaluation. It was fitted with skis and saw combat, although little is written about this.

The other original Sopwith Triplane is particularly rare, as it is one of only three Oakley & Smith–built tripes. Now at the RAF Museum and with serial number N5912, it began its museum experience at the Imperial War Museum after World War I. It was moved into storage in the early twenties and remained out of sight until the midthirties. Moved several times over the decades, N5912 spent some time in the Science Museum after being restored in the late sixties.

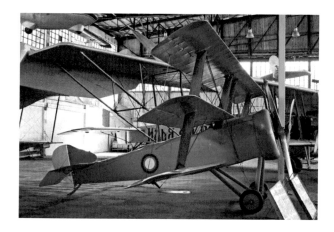

Sopwith Triplane—Monino

Donnet-Leveque

[Air Force Museum in Linkoping, Sweden]

Sweden's most popular and visited museum is the Vasa Museum, where an ancient sailing ship, literally out of the depths, sits before visitors as if it had been built yesterday. This masterpiece, salvaged in 1961, was built to be breathtaking in 1628, and indeed it still is, despite having sunk on its first foray. Not far from the Vasa's Stockholm dock location is Linkoping, where the Swedish Air Force Museum is found. At Linkoping, old wooden boats can also be found, but the original early aircraft collection is truly remarkable, with perhaps its greatest artifact the Donnet-Leveque Type A.

Donnet-Leveque was a French company formed by aviation pioneers Henri Leveque and Jerome Donnet but inspired by the aircraft designer Francois Denhaut. It was Denhaut who thought that Glenn Curtiss, although the true pioneer of early seaplanes, having first developed one in 1911, need not be the only manufacturer of such craft. Leveque was an automotive engine manufacturer, and Jerome Donnet was the money man, the source of capital. The new company, Donnett-Leveque, got its patent for the seaplane in 1912.

It's important to point out that a float plane and a flying boat are different, in that the float plane uses skis to float on the water and the flying boat is literally a hull with wings. In the case of the number ten Type A at the Swedish Air Force Museum, it utilizes both technologies, as it has a hull with wings but protects those wings with floats. Ultimately, one thousand Donnet-Leveque flying boats were built during the war years.

Although a Donnet-Leveque never participated in battle, discussion of early seaplanes would be incomplete without mention of the competition that in many ways motivated designers to keep their aviation interests with an eye toward the sea. The 1913 Schneider Trophy specifically created as a seaplane competition allowed the trophy to go and stay with the team that won three races in five years. At least 150 miles had to be traversed in a race format, with the winner to receive the Schneider Trophy itself, said to be worth 25,000 francs. The French millionaire Jacques Schneider, who inherited a fortune from metallurgy and the manufacture of rails, weapons, and iron ships, was inspired by the sight of Wilbur Wright's flights in France in 1908. Schneider, however, saw the ocean as the vast runway of the future, from which aircraft would land and take off without being encumbered by a lack of space.

Fortunately—and unfortunately—the Schneider Trophy competition was very popular, but not for the reason Jacques Schneider envisioned. The first race started in Monaco, with another race the following year, but World War I delayed further races until 1919. By this time, participation in the race saw countries looking for victory more for speed and less for innovation. It was impractical for entrepreneurs and club teams to compete against the world's national teams as Jacques had hoped. National pride was the fashion of the day, with no particular interest in developing a means of transportation for the masses via the oceans.

Having begun its restoration in 2010, the Donnet-Leveque found now at Linkoping had a paint scheme long ago that included images of fish scales covering the hull. It was called *Flygfisken*, which means "flying fish," and was so named by the man who purchased it in 1913, Carl Cederstrom. The aircraft was used at Cederstrom's flying school where he was known as the flying baron. With much ahead of Cederstrom and plenty to do with his company, Scandinavian Aviatik AB, Carl sold the Donnet-Leveque to the Swedish navy.

The Naval Aviation Service (NAS) gave the craft the designation of L11 and a serial number of 10. It served from the beginning of World War I to the end in 1918. After the war, the NAS donated the aircraft to the Maritime Museum in Stockholm, thus starting a long journey during which the aircraft's condition deteriorated over the years. Donnet-Leveque number 10 spent time with the Swedish National Museum of Science and Technology in the thirties and was placed in storage in the eighties, due to its poor condition.

Nyrop No. 3

[Museum of Science and Technology in Stockholm, Sweden]

Hjalmar Nyrop, born in 1885, was a Swedish engineer who was one of Sweden's founding fathers of early aviation. Although he died prematurely from injuries sustained in a flight in 1915, his contributions include building and flying the earliest aircraft in Scandinavia. In 1910, with partner Oskar Ask, Nyrop built an aircraft that he called the Nyrop I (also known as the Grasshopper) for the Swedish Aero Club's newly promoted air-week event.

Although Ask and Nyrop ended their business relationship quickly in 1911, three aircraft were built. After the split, Oskar Ask joined forces with Enoch Thulin. Thulin holds a special place in the history of Swedish aviation because his company, founded in 1914 and initially called Enoch Thulin's Aeroplanfabrik, was the first Swedish aircraft manufacturer. The company, later renamed and reorganized as AB Thulinverken, also built automobiles.

After the split between Ask and Nyrop, Nyrop continued alone and contracted to sell the last of the three aircraft he and Ask built to a brewery owner, O. E. Neumuller, who apparently had the financial wherewithal to purchase the aeroplane and then donate it to the Swedish navy. But he had some requirements before closing the deal. The brewer, who pursued some legitimacy for his interests in aviation, requested that the Swedish navy formally educate Lieutenant Olle Dahlbeck in an aviation school in England (The Grahame-White School). This requirement was agreed to, Dahlbeck got his aviator's license, and the Swedish navy got the Nyrop III, built in 1910. Dahlbeck ultimately was recognized for both the Swedish passenger-carrying and duration records.

To be fair, the Nyrop III was an underperformer and had a reputation as being difficult to fly. This is interesting, considering the Nyrop III, much like the other Nyrop aircraft, was constructed based on proven Blériot design details. The Nyrop III was finally retired in 1916, after being used for reconnaissance, but its original engine, a 50-horsepower Gnome, was removed in 1913 and placed in a Donnet-Lévêque flying boat. Today, Hjalmar's third Grasshopper Blériot Monoplane can be seen at the Museum of Science and Technology in Stockholm, Sweden. It is the oldest aircraft in Sweden.

Interestingly, the oldest *flying* aircraft in Sweden is also a Blériot XI and is found in the Museum of Science and Technology as well. Built by Enoch Thulin and called by some a "Thulin A," this original arrived at the museum at some point in the late twenties. It flew again in 2010 to celebrate the centennial of flight in Sweden. Mikael Carlson, who owns two original Blériots (Thulins) himself, worked for two years on the restoration.

Carlson, who pilots a 737 as his day job, started building model airplanes at an early age. It didn't take long for him to move to full-size aircraft. Carlson started by building what is considered a replica (has an original engine and some original parts) of the Swedish military aircraft, the Tummelisa biplane. He was twenty-three years old at the time.

Founded in 1924, the Museum of Science and Technology was created in large part to house the exhibits left over from the 1923 Gothenburg Exhibition (like a World's Fair). Most of the museum's possessions represent a period of technological growth that occurred in Sweden between the years of 1890 and 1930. There is an unusually large collection devoted to the production of steel and iron. However, there is great focus on chemistry, transportation, tools, and instruments.

The museum is just a forty-minute walk from downtown Stockholm and contains several gems for the early aviation enthusiast, such as an original Macchi M7, an Albatros SK.1, and a Bréguet BI.

Nieuport 28C

The engine company known as Nieuport-Duplex, which specialized in the manufacture of engine components, reorganized into a new company in 1909 called the Societe Generale d'Aero-locomotion. This new company focused its attention on the aviation industry, with specific attention to developing aircraft with enclosed fuselages, rather than the popular Wright and Blériot types of the time.

Company name changes came about and various lead designers were rotated out, but soon the Societe Anonyme des Etablissements Nieuport came under the leadership of Gustave Delage (no relationship to the automobile, the Delage) as the world moved toward war. The name Nieuport quickly became associated with the names of other successful fighter aircraft. Eddie Rickenbacker and Billy Bishop flew Nieuports for many of their early victories.

In 1918 with the introduction of the latest Nieuport, the 28, the war-weary but experienced French pilots simply considered the SPAD XIII a better machine. Because of this, the French flew the SPAD, and the Americans received the more available Nieuport 28s. Nearly 290 were purchased by the US military, at a price of $18,500 each; they were put into service as the first aircraft used by the American Expeditionary Forces.

The 95th Aero Squadron was first to fly the Nieuports in February 1918, followed quickly by the 94th. It was great to have American aviators in the air, but unfortunately, these first delivered Nieuport 28s were unarmed aircraft. Still, they were flown out across the front lines as a show of force and a morale booster.

The 94th flew its first armed patrol on March 28, and not long after, on April 14, Lt. Campbell scored the first kill for an American unit when he downed a Pfalz D.IIIa near his base. It's worth noting that Douglass Campbell made his first kill with one machine gun rather than the usual two-gun configuration. Campbell later became the second air service ace and the first American trained pilot to shoot down a fifth enemy aircraft over Lironville, France, on May 31, 1918. Such achievement earned him the Distinguished Service Cross and the Croix de Guerre avec Palme from the French military. He ended the war with six victories.

Hanging from the ceiling at the Museum der Schweizerischen Fliegertruppe in Dubendorf, Switzerland, is an original Nieuport 28. Originally assigned serial number N.6212 and flown by American Lieutenant James F. Ashinden of the 147th Aero Squadron, this Nieuport made an emergency landing in Switzerland, which was about 130 miles away from Ashinden's Aerodrome in Toul, France.

The aircraft was not badly damaged and consequently was repaired and kept by the Swiss. It was used by the Swiss air force with a reissued serial number 607 and used as a trainer until 1925, when it was placed in long storage.

The Museum der Schweizerischen Fliegertruppe, also referred to as the Dubendorf Air Force Center Museum, is not far from Zurich and hosts many original aircraft, including a Hanriot HD-1 and a Blériot XI.

Sopwith Snipe

Sir Thomas Sopwith died at the age of 101, of what his son described as old age after a marvelous life. According to his obituary, Thomas Sopwith was eighteen when he learned to fly a balloon. "By 22 he had taught himself to fly an airplane and held Britain's 31st aviator certificate. Sir Thomas raised money for his first airplane manufacturing company by stunt flying. He won a prize of $4,000 for pioneering flight across the English Channel. In the next few years he made more than $28,000 by stunt-flying around Boston, New York and Chicago and by 1912 was able to establish the Sopwith Aviation Company." With great success often comes great fortune; Thomas Sopwith was wealthy enough in later years to finance two attempts to win the America's Cup in yachting, neither of which he won.

The Sopwith Aviation Company ultimately built sixteen thousand aircraft for the Great War effort. Six thousand were Camels. Always one to name his designs creatively, Sopwith aircraft types had names like Camel, Dolphin, Buffalo, Pup, and Salamander. Continuing this naming tradition, the Sopwith Snipe, named after the long-billed shorebird, was designed to replace the Sopwith Camel. It was only slightly faster, however, even when modified with an engine with one hundred horsepower more than originally planned.

The Snipe was much easier to fly than the Camel and thus was a significant improvement for one of the last of the rotary engine fighter types. Ultimately, there were only about one hundred Snipes delivered in time for the end of the war.

Most notable of the Snipe's successes occurred while it was under the piloting skills of Major W. B. Barker, a Canadian pilot who singlehandedly fought off fifteen Fokker D.VIIs. Although severely wounded, he shot down three of the enemy planes. This earned him the Victoria Cross. Barker remains the most decorated Canadian warrior of all time. Today, his bullet riddled fuselage E8102 can be seen at the Canadian War Museum.

One of only two complete examples that survive today, the Snipe displayed at the Canada Aviation and Space Museum in Rockcliffe on the outskirts of Ottawa has serial number E6938. (The other is in the Smithsonian's National Air and Space Museum, donated by the late Cole Palen of the Old Rhinebeck Aerodrome.)

Rockcliffe's Snipe is a Nieuport-built machine manufactured in 1918 that more than likely served overseas. The actor and former RFC pilot Reginald Denny brought the Snipe to California, where it was used in several films. The Sopwith was carefully restored to flying condition by Jack Canary in the late fifties and later sold to the Canada Aviation and Space Museum. E6938 last flew in 1967 at Air Force Day celebrations, when it was damaged. Today it is restored for static display.

Fokker DVII

The skies over the western front were quickly being controlled by the Allies in late 1917, forcing Germany to reevaluate the single-seat fighters being produced. A test trial was arranged, for which thirty manufacturers each designed and built an aircraft. From this competition, held in Berlin in January 1918, production of the Fokker DVII was born.

Although the name on the nameplate is Fokker, Anthony Fokker was really a natural and talented test pilot, who excelled at "feeling" the modifications that needed to be implemented on a newly designed aircraft. On the other hand, perhaps the true design talent for the Fokker organization was Reinhold Platz. One of the best examples of Platz's genius was the Fokker V.11, which was the designation given to the Berlin test plane later designated DVII.

Once in a battle sky, the Fokker DVII became known and feared for its ability to stay positioned under an enemy plane without stalling. This would enable the Fokker pilot to riddle the allied aircraft with bullets in its vulnerable underbelly. Many historians consider the DVII to be one of the finest fighter aircraft to participate from either side during World War I. It famously was called out by name for destruction within the armistice documents themselves. Because the Germans were forced to give up the remaining aircraft that survived the war—nearly eight hundred pristine planes—many were destroyed and many were given away as war prizes to various countries, but some were effectively repurposed. It has been said that Anthony Fokker himself smuggled 220 DVIIs to his home country of the Netherlands.

Interestingly, World War I was not the only war in which the Fokker DVII was in use. In fact, the DVII's battle history had a few more additions. They include use in the Hungarian-Romanian War of 1919 and the Polish-Soviet War of 1919–1921. In 1919, Poland's air force consisted of mostly German and Austrian aircraft. Along with the Fokker DVII, there were the Oeffag D.III and the Albatros J.I, captured from the former central Axis powers. Most notably, these now-Polish aircraft conducted wartime operations around the city known then as Lwow. (The Polish-Soviet War ended with the Treaty of Riga).

Besides Germany's neighbors, the United States received more than one hundred of these spoils of war. Navy and army units replaced many of the DVII's 160-horsepower Mercedes D.III engines with Liberty L-6 engines. The DVII at the Canada Aviation and Space Museum was built by the Fokker Flugzeug-Werke GmbH in 1918 and was one of the planes that the United States acquired. Eventually considered surplus and then sold, this DVII, serial number 10347/18, was yet another aircraft used in the movies. The serial number revealed that this particular aircraft was produced so late in the war that it was likely taken directly from the factory at the end of hostilities. In this particular case, 10347/18 was employed by *Hell's Angels*, the Howard Hughes blockbuster. *Hell's Angels*, which took three years to film and had the highest movie budget of all time up to that point ($4 million), used 150 aircraft and was shot as a silent film. Once sound became the norm, Hughes had to recreate the film with sound. It opened to rave reviews, but the film was so expensive to make that it never made a profit.

Canada's Aviation and Space Museum acquired its Fokker in 1971 in need of a propeller and engine. Both of these were eventually received as donations in the midseventies. However, a full restoration of this gem has yet to be completed.

Nieuport 28 C.1

[National Aeronautics Museum in Buenos Aires, Argentina]

As we have seen, not all aircraft displays are standard or even similar. This is an understatement when it comes to the remains of a Nieuport 28 C.1 found in a glass case at the National Aeronautics Museum in Buenos Aires, Argentina.

The museum was founded in 1960 mostly as a collection of, and dedicated to, the Argentine air force. Initially located at an outside venue known as the Aeroparque Jorge Newbery, where weather affected the sustainability of the collection, it was moved in the 2000s to the Morón Airport and Air Base, where Argentina's first international airport was established and where hangars were available to house under a roof the many valuables that make up the museum today. Notable aircraft in the collection include an Ansaldo SVA that may be in storage awaiting eventual restoration, an original balloon basket used by the Argentine aviation pioneer Eduardo Newbery (brother of Jorge Newbery), and the remnants of the aforementioned Nieuport flown by Benjamin Matienzo.

Matienzo was a courageous pilot who dared to consider crossing the Andes Mountains by aircraft. The mountain range that separates Chile and Argentina is six hundred meters high, or almost twenty thousand feet. Of the many feats in aviation before and just after World War I, the Andes crossing was a tempting but extremely dangerous challenge. Benjamin Matienzo was a lieutenant in the Argentine military and a pilot, having graduated from the Argentine Military Aviation School in 1918.

It was May 1919 when three pilots attempted the flight at about the same time. Pilots Zanni, Parodi, and Matienzo all took off from Tamarinds Airfield. Not long after, both Zanni and Parodi returned safely with fuel and engine issues. No word was received from Matienzo, and after several hours, then days, it seemed inevitable that something tragic had occurred in the mountains. With the assistance of Chilean officials, a search was conducted on both sides of the Andes with no results.

It wasn't until November that a small search team found Matienzo's body. It was clear whose remains they were, as a ring found on the body revealed the initials HM. It was also pretty clear that Matienzo did not die in the crash, as evidence showed he had walked a great distance in bad weather before succumbing to the elements. There have been reports that there were bullets missing from Matienzo's gun, suggesting suicide in such dire circumstances, but this may be unfounded speculation.

More than thirty years later in 1950, mountain patrols found Matiezo's Nieuport 28 C.1 at an altitude of forty-five hundred meters (14,700 feet). Today, the National Aeronautics Museum respectfully honors Lieutenant Matienzo with an encased shrine of what was left of the aviator's aircraft.

Putting this tragedy and the length of time it took to discover Matienzo's plane in perspective, one must remember that it was just recently (February 2015), and with modern technology, that the wreckage of a Chilean DC-3 was found in the Andes at ten thousand feet. This was the well-documented 1961 crash of the plane carrying the members of a Chilean soccer team. (This is not the 1972 crash that inspired the book *Alive*, by Piers Paul Read.)

Nieuport 28 C.1—National Aeronautics Mus.

Hanriot HD-1

[Aeronautical Museum of the Ecuadorian Air Force in Quito, Ecuador]

Quito is the capital city of the South American country of Ecuador. Much of the western portion of South America is lined by the Andes Mountains. As mentioned in these pages, the Andes is a formidable challenge to cross at most points. It was first crossed by aircraft in 1918 by Argentine Luis Candelaria, yet the Ecuadorian segment of the mountains had yet to be traversed by a powered aeroplane. This all came to a victorious end on November 4, 1920, when Italian pilot Elia Liut crossed the Andes in just an hour's flight from the coastal city of Guayaquil to the mountain town of Cuenca, with an altitude of eighty-two hundred feet.

The heroic deed of Liut—who quickly became an Ecuadorian hero known as the "Andean Condor"—begins back in 1920, when he moved from Italy to Ecuador at the request of Miguel Valverde Letamendi (Ecuadorian Consul to Italy, based in Rome). This strategy was a coordinated attempt to develop the science of aviation in Ecuador. At the same time, the owner of one of Ecuador's oldest and most respected newspapers, *El Telegrafo*, funded the journey of Liut's airplane to Ecuador from Italy. Once the Macchi-licensed Hanriot HD-1 arrived, it was to be used in a city-to-city promotional tour, with the newspaper's name printed on the side of the aircraft.

Liut was born in Italy, moved with his family to Argentina when he was eight, and then returned to Italy at the age of sixteen. He earned his pilot's license in 1915 just after World War I started and honorably contributed in many aerial missions on various fronts.

It's important to point out that crossing the Andes was not necessarily part of the original Liut mission. It seems that when the notion of sending the Italian pilot's crated Hanriot to the mountain city of Cuenca by train, then on the backs of men and horses for the last leg into the mountains, was raised, Elia Liut proposed a flight straight to Cuenca. Once the Ecuadoran government approved the flight, a legend was created.

In Quito today, the Aeronautical Museum of the Ecuadorian Air Force owns and displays Liut's Hanriot, dressed still as the El Telegrafo billboard. Donated to the Ecuadoran government in 1922 by the owner of El Telegrafo, Jose Abel Castillo, the plane, originally built in around 1918 as part of wartime production, saw service as a trainer for the military. Some sources suggest that the plane is in need of a full restoration and that the original Clerget has been changed.

Note: Getting to great altitude has always been a sought-after achievement in aviation. This was especially true in the early days of flight, simply because of its inherent danger. When a pilot seeks a higher altitude, the dynamic pressure decreases. With a wing size that is constant, an aircraft must fly at a higher lift coefficient by increasing the angle of attack. Each aircraft had a different "ceiling," and in 1920, a specific airplane such as the Hanriot HD-1 maintained unknown ceiling limits. One must keep in mind also that with increased altitude comes decreased air speed, so engine size (horsepower) is critical.

SPAD S.XIII

A native of Arizona, Frank Luke was a Congressional Medal of Honor recipient for his courageous acts as a fighter pilot in World War I. Although born in Germany, in 1917 he enlisted in the aviation section, US Signal Corps. Sent for training to both California and Texas, he was made second lieutenant in March 1918 before being deployed to France for further training. It was that July when he was assigned to the 27th Aero Squadron.

An amateur boxer before the war, Luke had a reputation of being too self-assured, which led to an unpopular status among his peers. He tended to fly as a lone wolf, which did not endear him to his squadron, although it did bode well for the sort of patrols that were among the most dangerous. Balloon busting was a great hazard for many reasons, not the least of which was the extraordinary defense placed around German balloons in the form of artillery and riflemen. Throughout 1917 and 1918, German observation balloons supplied their ground forces with valuable troop positions. Keeping these balloons in the air was a priority, so the Allies made it a priority to shoot them down.

Frank Luke and his friend Lt. Joseph Frank Wehner volunteered to hunt these targets despite the fortified antiaircraft emplacements. Both flying SPADs, Luke and Wehner enjoyed a great deal of success and became quite well known on the front. Such bravery comes with great cost, as both Wehner and Luke eventually died in separate incidents hunting the "gas bags." Many stories, perhaps a bit exaggerated, were told of Luke's heroic last flight. One story had him, after landing his SPAD, shooting seven German soldiers on the ground with his last pistol rounds just before he succumbed to his mortal injury. Although this is unlikely, we do know that Frank Luke was an exceedingly brave warrior who made a critical mistake in his last flight. He flew where enemy ground fire could reach him. He was struck by one bullet. (A similar error was made by Manfred Baron von Richtofen, the Red Baron, while chasing the Canadian pilot Roy Brown at low altitude.)

Luke will forever be remembered for a seventeen-day stretch in September 1918 when, in only ten missions, he shot down fourteen enemy balloons and, based on differing sources, shot down a further four to seven aircraft. In dedication to Luke's war success, the city of Phoenix acquired an original SPAD XIII that is reported to have been assembled from three original SPADs and is made up of about 80 percent original parts; it was restored in 2007 by the experienced and well-respected firm of GossHawk Unlimited. Based conveniently in Arizona, GossHawk assisted with the fabric work on another war survivor, a Pfalz D.XII now at the Museum of Flight in Seattle.

Visitors to the Phoenix Sky Harbor International Airport will see the SPAD XIII hanging in terminal 3. The aircraft displays the markings of the 27th Squadron of the First Pursuit Group and sports an original water-cooled Hispano-Suiza engine with top speeds of 138 miles per hour. It should be noted that, during World War I, the SPAD S.XIII was greatly criticized for unreliable engines. An official report stated that two-thirds of the 200-horsepower SPADs were out of use at any one time due to engine problems. However, during the war, the SPAD S.XIII was flown by many a famous pilot. These include the French super-aces Georges Guynemer and Rene Fonck, Italian ace

Francesco Baracca and America's best, Eddie Rickenbacker, who scored twenty-six confirmed victories.

The XIII was active for most squadrons until September 1918, when in some cases, the underrated and rarely mentioned Sopwith Dolphin replaced the SPAD. In the end, approximately eighty-five hundred SPAD S.XIIIs were built, with orders for several thousand more canceled due to the ending of hostilities.

Hanriot HD-1

The French-built and French-designed Hanriot HD-1 was used by Belgian and Italian forces in 1916 during World War I. The French preferred the SPAD VII, allowing the Hanriots to find their way into the hands of Allies, where they proved to be effective in battle. The Hanriot was a bit underpowered with its 110 LeRhone rotary engine, but it was highly maneuverable. One of the reasons for its agility and ability to ascend quickly was its lightness, due in part to carrying only one Vickers machine gun. The HD-1 was considered reliable and safe, which were greatly appreciated assets in 1916, and therefore it was a popular airplane among its pilots.

The Hanriot HD-1 sprang from the mind of Emile Dupont, who worked for Rene Hanriot's manufacturing company known as Aeroplanes Hanriot et Cie. Rene, a noted race-car driver and powerboat pilot, began his aviation career in 1907 with a design that was similar to the Blériot XI. He borrowed many of the Blériot's features. He and Emile did the same with the HD-1 a decade later by borrowing from the Sopwith 1.5 Strutter design. Rene's son Marcel was as passionate about aviation as his father and became the youngest certified pilot in the world at age fifteen. Marcel later joined his father in the manufacturing of aircraft after having been wounded while serving as a bomber crew for the French in World War I.

The Hanriot HD-1 was flown by several famous pilots during the Great War, including Willy Copens, the famous Belgian ace best known for his balloon busting, and the Italian ace Silvio Scaroni with twenty-six victories. However, no HD-1 pilot is more famous than Charles Nungesser. The Iron Man, as he was sometimes called because of the many times he was wounded while flying, was known for his courage and his remarkable skill as a pilot. This skill resulted in forty-six kills and a rank of third among all French aces.

The Hanriot HD-1 at the Planes of Fame museum in Chino, California, is of particular interest because it was Nungesser's own plane, which he brought to the United States from France after World War I. Not known for his shyness, Charles Nungesser participated in the movie *The Sky Raiders* in 1925 with this Hanriot HD-1 and promoted the picture by doing fly-bys in the cities where the film was playing. Sadly, in May 1927, Nungesser and Major Francois Coli left from Paris, attempting to cross the Atlantic east to west. They were last seen off the coast of Ireland and never seen again. Search efforts concluded with the determination that both men were lost at sea, all of this just twelve days before Charles Lindbergh's successful crossing of the Atlantic. In all of these years, the only potential clues to the fate of Coli and Nungesser are pieces of wreckage found in 1961 in lobster baskets by fisherman off the coast of Maine near Cliff Island. A large piece of an airplane fuselage was found and eventually sent to Paris but never conclusively identified as a remnant of the *Oiseau Blanc*, Nungesser's lost plane.

The Hanriot HD-1, parked in Southern California until 1929, was forfeited to pay the storage bills. In an auction, Californian Jim Granger purchased the plane and used it in movies such as *Hell's Angels* and *Wings* and even had it parked for a time in front of Grauman's Chinese Theatre (now called Mann's Chinese Theatre) in Los Angeles. The plane was often parked in public places for all to enjoy up close. This resulted in vandalism on several occasions, including most notably the cutting out of Nungesser's iconic insignia, the black heart with skull and candlesticks. Another insignia was created and painstakingly sewn back in place by hand.

The Hanriot was placed in storage by Granger from 1933 until 1951, when it was purchased by Ed Maloney, the founder of the Planes of Fame Museum that now displays it. When it comes to aircraft preservation, few organizations can equal the effort and ambition of the Planes of Fame Museum. It is a well-known and highly respected institution in Southern California, where some of the rarest air antiques from all eras can be found. These include a B-17, a Yak-18, a Hawker Hurricane, a Mitsubishi Zero, a P-51 Mustang, and many more. Since 1957, Ed Maloney, with the assistance of family members, has compiled a collection of 150 aircraft housed at two locations: Chino and Valle Airport in Arizona.

California was the aircraft manufacturing hub of the United States for much of the twentieth century. It is ironic that, without preservationists like the Maloneys to find, restore, preserve, and feature these museum gems, the rich California aviation heritage might have gone overlooked and underestimated.

Hanriot HD-1—Planes of Fame

Deperdussin Militaire

[San Diego Air and Space Museum in San Diego, CA, USA]

The Société pour les Apparelis was an aircraft manufacturer in France that was begun in 1909 by Armand Deperdussin and his engineers, Louis Bechereau and Andre Herbemont. Called Aeroplanes Deperdussin at first, the company gained acclaim for early racing monoplanes with a sleek and stable design in 1910. It was this racing design that won the Gordon Bennett Trophy in 1912 and 1913 for raising the world speed record for aircraft to 130 miles per hour (210 kilometers per hour).

Armand Deperdussin was quite a businessman. Never to be confused with the aircraft inventors who loved the simple notion of manned flight, Deperdussin saw the potential fortune to be made in the manufacture of aircraft. Among many career endeavors, including selling chocolate and singing in a night club, he eventually made a fortune brokering silk to Parisian dress shops.

Deperdussin, who began with French contracts to build aeroplanes, moved on to accommodate the needs of the Russians. Later accused of fraud and embezzlement, which Deperdussin eventually confessed to, he ended up with a prison term. This opened the door for Louis Blériot, a competitor at the time, to essentially take over Deperdussin's company. Even the company's acronym remained unchanged under Blériot. Blériot's SPAD (now formally called Société Pour L'Aviation et ses Dérivés) went on to produce some of the most famous aircraft used in World War I.

A canard design was Armand Deperdussin's first attempt at establishing a viable style of plane to manufacture. As discussed earlier the *canard*, which means "duck" in French, had the tailplane ahead of the main lifting surfaces rather than behind them. Chosen often as a design for early flyers, the canard style usually included a heavy landing gear perfect for an aircraft's landing…if it flew at all. But the canard design turned out to be unsuccessful. From this initial failure, as is so often the case, Deperdussin adjusted the design dramatically and ended up with the familiar clean-cut mono/tractor style. A tractor configuration simply means the propeller is in front. This contrasted greatly with the common pusher style of the time period.

The Deperdussin on display at the San Diego Air and Space Museum in Balboa Park is a rare 1911 Military Type. This was discovered after careful inspection, as it was thought to be a C Type for many years. This particular aircraft had been a part of a few legendary collections, including the Jean Salis Collection in Paris and then the Wings & Wheels Museum (Orlando, Florida), whose contents were auctioned by Christie's on August 6, 1982. The generosity of several foundations allowed the San Diego Air and Space Museum to acquire the Deperdussin at this auction.

The Wings & Wheels Museum was forced to liquidate its collection because it lost its lease, which was held by the Orlando Airport Authority. Museums tend not to be overly profitable endeavors. There were more attractive lease options for the airport authority to entertain. Interestingly, the auction brought in $350,000 for a 1934 Packard Phaeton (a car), but an original 1917 Sopwith Camel sold for only $120,000. The Wings & Wheels Museum was made up of three smaller collections: the original W&W Museum in Santee, South Carolina; the Dolph Overton collection; and the Aeroflex (New Jersey) collection.

Standard J-1

Americans have the most, and arguably the greatest, aviation museums in the world. To see the best, one only must travel thousands of miles from one coast to the other; there are literally hundreds of collections along the way. If the Smithsonian National Air and Space Museum in Washington, DC, and the National Museum of the US Air Force in Dayton, Ohio, are America's best, then surely the San Diego Air and Space Museum in California wins the bronze medal. (Understandably, there may be some disagreement in Pensacola, Chino, New York State, Seattle...)

With incredible restoration capabilities found in two locations, one in San Diego's Balboa Park and the other at Gillespie Field, the SDASM enjoys the skills of volunteers, many of whom worked in Southern California's vast aerospace industry. The facilities contain a large archive of books, records, and photos for research into the details of old aircraft. It is this data source that leaves the SDASM in the winner's circle.

Affiliated with the Smithsonian Institution as of 2005, the SDASM unfortunately was the subject of one of America's worst museum fires. In 1978, a fire started in the museum's electrical building in Balboa Park. Nearly sixty replicas and some original aircraft were lost. Along with lost aircraft were destroyed engines and thousands of books. Loss estimates were considered to be in the range of $10 million. Just after the fire, the San Diego community came out in great numbers to assist in salvaging whatever could be restored. The museum remained in temporary headquarters for two years in the restored Ford building, part of the 1935 World's Fair held in Balboa Park, officially called the 1935 California Pacific International Exhibition. Slowly filling the museum halls were aircraft built by volunteers or originals lent by the Smithsonian National Air and Space Museum. Unbelievably, the tragic fire turned out to be the work of an arsonist.

One-of-a-kind losses include

- a Beecraft Wee Bee, the world's lightest aircraft, and her sister craft the Queen Bee;

- a reproduction of the Spirit of Saint Louis built in 1967 by some of the same people who built the original; and

- the International Aerospace Hall of Fame.

Today, however, the collection thrives. The early aircraft collection is full of fine originals, including a Deperdussin, a SPAD, and a Nieuport. The museum also exhibits two of America's most well-loved early aeroplanes: a Curtiss JN-4D and a Standard J-1. Both were trainers for the military, and both were probably better known for their postwar barnstorming activities.

The Standard Company started as Sloan Company, which began in 1916 in New Jersey. Quickly changing its name to Standard, it was one of the US military's first aircraft suppliers. Standard produced the H-2 and H-3 for army use and the H-4 float plane for the navy. Standard produced approximately eight hundred J-1s for the military but failed to impress anyone asked to fly the aircraft, as it was underpowered and therefore dangerous. This perception/reality resulted in an abundance of J-1s being stored instead of used. However, after the war, surplus J-1s were easily and inexpensively available. Once the J-1 was reequipped with a Hispano-Suiza engine, much of the danger of flying the plane dissipated. The J-1 had no brakes, which was in and of itself a danger that was often exploited by the shenanigans of barnstormers.

Originally part of a purchase made in the early fifties, the SDASM's Standard J-1 was part of a collection of antique aircraft at Roosevelt Field on Long Island, New York. When the decision was made to build a shopping mall where the field stood, at least nine World War I–era airplanes were put up for sale. The Smithsonian quickly purchased three of them, but an astute and ambitious Cole Palen of the Old Rhinebeck Aerodrome purchased six others, including a SPAD XIII, an Avro 504K, a Curtiss Jenny, a Standard J-l, an Aeromarine 39B, and a Sopwith Snipe.

The Standard J-1 was traded in the sixties to Tallmantz Aviation in Chino, California, for an original Nieuport 28. From there, the Standard J-1 with serial number 5083 was acquired by the San Diego Air and Space Museum.

Blériot XI

[New England Air Museum in Windsor Locks, CT, USA]

By now most of us know the story of Louis Blériot's famous flight on July 25, 1909. He crossed the English Channel from Calais, France, to the English cliffs of Dover. This earned him the humble amount of £1,000, but more important, it garnered the attention of the world and led all to believe that aircraft might have far-reaching uses past simple sport. So endearing was this particular Blériot that it never flew again; it was put on display at Selfridges department store in London, later displayed outside the offices of the French newspaper *Le Matin*, and finally purchased by the Musée des Arts et Metiers in Paris, where it can be seen today.

So endearing was the design of Blériot's aircraft, it quickly became the most common aircraft of its day. Priced reasonably at 12,000 francs, it was half the price of the competition and consequently manufactured in large numbers by Blériot's company and by licensed companies in Italy and England. In 1911, just two years after the crossing, there were at least five hundred Blériot's in the hands of new aviators. On both sides of the Atlantic, unlicensed machines were being built as well. These were effectively copies of the Blériot design, built in backyards and garages.

At the New England Aviation Museum (NEAM) at Bradley Airport in Windsor Locks, Connecticut, there sits one of these homebuilt Blériots. Ernest C. Hall of Warren, Ohio, built and flew this aircraft until 1917, when it was damaged. The NEAM reports that the plane, given to the museum as a gift by the United Technologies Corporation, "had several owners and was restored to flight status by Shirley Wardle in 1966. He flew it until 1975. Wardle installed a 65-horsepower Continental engine but saved all the original parts. It was damaged again in a tornado which hit the museum and was restored using the original parts including the rare Detroit Aero engine."

Note: Another original (1911) Ernest Hall–built Blériot is found at the National Museum of the US Air Force in Dayton, Ohio.

Ernest C. Hall is probably best known for his fifty-plus years of aviation involvement. This is fascinating, considering the newness of the industry and the many turns the industry took over the years, civil and military. Having lived in the former home of the Packard (automobile) family, Hall spent years of his youth building and flying various flying contraptions: gliders and the Blériot variants he has been identified with. Sources point out that, although Hall copied the Blériot design, he added enough differences to be considered an aircraft designer himself.

In 1913, Ernest Hall was given the opportunity to teach the art of flying as an instructor for the Curtiss Exhibition Company in Virginia. This was a treasured position for an early flyer, because the Curtiss Exhibition Company was established to promote aviation, Curtiss products, and the Curtiss Flight School. It toured the country, demonstrating the capabilities of Curtiss biplanes, such as loop-the-loops, spirals, etc. Although Hall fared well in this organization, the intrinsic danger of demonstration flying at this time cannot be overlooked. For example, Cromwell Dixon, the world's youngest licensed aviator and a Curtiss student, died in Seattle; Eugene B. Ely, who worked for Curtiss in San Diego, died in 1911 while performing aerial stunts. Julia Clark, known as the "bird girl," graduated from the San Diego Curtiss school and died just one month later, and the world-renowned Lincoln Beechey, the greatest exhibition flyer of his day and graduate of the 1911 Curtiss school class, died when his plane crashed into the San Francisco Bay in 1915.

Despite this, Ernest Hall, known as Ernie, lived to the age of seventy-five, unscathed in the career he had chosen. In 1915 he established a flying school of his own at Conneaut, Pennsylvania.

Ernest Hall's experiences were all part of civil aviation until he decided to join the aviation section of the Army Signal Corps at McCook Field in Dayton, Ohio, where he served as an experienced flight instructor. Eventually he was transferred to Call Field at Wichita Falls, Texas, where he was credited with training five hundred young aviators for possible action in the First World War in Europe. Ultimately, Hall was recognized for his contributions and appointed director of the Ohio Bureau of Aeronautics. We'd be remiss if we did not mention that Hall was a member of the highly regarded Early Birds, an organization of pioneers whose membership required that they had flown solo before December 17, 1916.

Wiseman-Cooke

[National Postal Museum in Washington, DC, USA]

The Smithsonian National Air and Space Museum at any given time has a number of its aircraft out on loan to other institutions, organizations, or museums. Although the National Postal Museum is part of the Smithsonian, it too features some of the borrowed NASM aircraft. The Wiseman-Cooke aircraft is such a treasure.

Back in 1911 when practical uses for the aeroplane were still being contemplated, Fred Wiseman, an automobile racer and auto-repair foreman, took to the air to deliver the mail. He was formally sanctioned for the task by the US Postal Service to bring meaning to a trip that was mostly promotional. The flight was a twenty-mile trek in California, from Petaluma to Santa Rosa, and consisted of the delivery of one or two letters from the Petaluma postmaster to the Santa Rosa postmaster. Apparently the mayors of the two cities drafted similar correspondence.

Taking two days due to some technical problems that resulted in a forced landing, the adventure employed an aircraft built by Wiseman and his partners in 1909. The aircraft was featured in fairs and other events before its airmail fame and was very similar to what one would see in use by the Wrights or Glenn Curtiss in other parts of the country. In fact, the Wiseman-Cooke was a copy of the Curtiss design. The name Cooke was added later when Weldon Cooke purchased the airplane from Wiseman and tweaked the design further. Unfortunately, Cooke, using another of his aircraft, died in a crash in 1914 at the age of thirty. By this time, Wiseman had returned to the safer environment of the auto business.

The Fred Wiseman story is an important one because it helped bring an interest in aviation to the US West Coast. In what is now Sonoma County Airport in California, Wiseman built and tested his airplane on what was then the Laughlin Ranch. The ranch featured plenty of open space and very few obstacles to hit. Wiseman, who was in his midtwenties, used a V-8 engine built by Al Hall, who later was responsible for the groundbreaking aircraft engine known as the Hall-Scott. The original Hall engine in the Wiseman-Cooke aircraft was modified, as it was underpowered. This lack of power resulted in the aircraft's inability to turn in the air, so the Wiseman-Cooke was only able to fly in a straight line early on. It had to land and be rotated around by the ground crew for the short hop back the other way.

The original Wiseman-Cooke exhibited at the National Postal Museum was restored by the Smithsonian's Garber Facility in 1985. It was Weldon Cooke's brother, Robert, who preserved the Wiseman-Cooke aircraft after Weldon's death. The aircraft was kept in storage in Oakland, California, until 1933, when Robert Cooke allowed the Oakland Port Authority to display the plane at the Oakland Airport.

Around 1947, the National Air Museum was aggressively expanding the national collection. This strategy included acquiring significant US aircraft for its halls. Paul Garber, curator of the National Air Museum, approached the families for their consent to donate the Wiseman-Cooke aircraft to the Smithsonian Institution. They agreed, and the Wiseman-Cooke along with another early original, the Maupin-Lanteri Black Diamond (also flown often by Cooke), were sent into storage in Washington, DC, to await restoration at the hands of Smithsonian historians.

Ultimately, the Smithsonian restored the Wiseman-Cooke, but the Black Diamond was restored by the Hiller Air Museum in San Carlos, California, for the NASM.

Wiseman-Cooke—National Postal Museum

Fokker DVII

[The Smithsonian National Air and Space Museum in Washington, DC, USA]

Anthony Fokker, not known as a good student but born with a natural talent for mechanics, was only twenty years old when he founded his first aviation company in the German city of Wiesbaden. Fokker was not German but Dutch, having been raised in the Netherlands. He moved to Germany at his father's behest to formalize his education as an auto mechanic at a top school, Bingen Technical School.

But aviation was of greater interest to Fokker, who quickly switched gears and focused his education and his efforts on designing and creating aeroplanes. His first creation was the Fokker Spin 1, built in 1910. It wasn't long before the first Spin was crashed by Fokker's business associate Franz von Daum, but the engine was still in working condition and was quickly placed in Spin 2. It was in this second Spin example that Anthony Fokker learned to fly and subsequently earned his pilot's license.

Although this second Spin was destroyed (by Daum once again), the ambitious and intelligent Fokker built a third Spin and flew it around the tower of the Sint Bavokerk church in Haarlem in the Netherlands. He gained a good bit of fame with this flight, as it was timed expertly with Queen Wilhelmina's birthday on August 31, 1911. Fokker used his notoriety to move to Germany, where he secured a contract to build the Fokker M.1 through the M.4 for the German military. These types were based on the Spin design.

One of Anthony Fokker's greatest contributions to the Axis war effort was the synchronized machine gun, which had a trigger mechanism timed with the spinning of the propeller. This invention put Germany ahead of the Allies in the air war early on. Ultimately Germany's confidence in Fokker allowed him to design other aircraft that were to change the war, at least in the air. As discussed in earlier chapters, Anthony Fokker's DVII design was so effective that individual airplanes were accounted for at the end of the war and classified for either destruction or war reparation to victorious countries.

The DVII at the Smithsonian National Air and Space Museum in Washington is an Albatros licensed built aircraft that was fighting with Jasta 65. It was captured completely intact, as described here by NASM: "On November 9, 1918, two days before the end of the war, Lieutenant Heinz Freiherr von Beaulieu-Marconnay landed the NASM Fokker D.VII at a forward American airfield being used by the 95th Aero Squadron, near Verdun. The pilot and airplane were captured by three American officers before Beaulieu-Marconnay could set fire to his aircraft. It is uncertain whether or not Beaulieu-Marconnay was lost and mistakenly landed at what he thought was a German airfield (as he claimed), or simply surrendered, knowing that the war would soon be over and fabricated the story."

This particular airplane was saved from destruction and brought to the United States, where it was presented to the Smithsonian by the US War Department in 1920. Fokker DVII serial number 4635/18, marked U.10, underwent a complete restoration by NASM in 1961.

Nieuport 28

The Nieuport 28 appeared on the front in France during World War I in 1918. The French-built aircraft was especially helpful to the American fliers, as there was a shortage of combat-effective planes ready to fly. The Americans were new to the fight, having entered the war formally in April 1917, but were left with no supply of their own manufactured aircraft; a steady delivery of aircraft was promised but never materialized before the war ended.

Fortunately, the SPAD XIII was already in use and seen as the Allied workhorse when the Nieuport 28 appeared and became the first aircraft in use at the front by American squadrons. Unlike the Nieuport 17, which was considered underpowered, the Nieuport 28 possessed the powerful 160-horsepower Gnome Monosoupape rotary engine as well as dual machine guns.

The US 94th and 95th Squadrons began their campaigns with the Nieuport 28. Although the 28 was only used by American pilots for several months, many famous pilots cut their teeth at the controls. Douglass Campbell, Eddie Rickenbacker, and Quentin Roosevelt, the son of former president Theodore Roosevelt, all flew the Nieuport 28 in combat. It should be noted that Quentin Roosevelt died in battle while flying the Nieuport 28.

Unlike so many other aircraft types used in the actual Great War conflict, perhaps fifty or more Nieuport 28s were shipped back to the United States after the war. They were used in many capacities while in US military possession, most notably as a test craft for shipboard landings. The Nieuport 28 style became closely associated with the typical look of a World War I Allied aircraft, and for this reason, Hollywood had a role for this type in many films. The 28s were used in films such as *Dawn Patrol*; its sequel, *Ace of Aces*; *Men with Wings*; and *The Lafayette Escadrille*. So evocative an image of a dogfighter was the Nieuport 28 that when the supply of original aircraft became scarce, reproductions were created specifically to satisfy the call of the film industry.

A gentleman named Claude Flagg designed a reproduction airplane called the Garland-Lincoln LF-1. Garland-Lincoln, which was the manufacturer, produced three of these in Glendale, California, to be used as stand-ins for Nieuport 28s. The Garland-Lincolns were built at the height of Hollywood's interest in World War I aviation.

The Smithsonian NASM's Nieuport 28 carries serial numbers 6497, 7103, 7226, 6465, and 6432—yes, there are five different serial numbers found on different parts of the aircraft. Only a true Sherlock Holmes could piece together a bit of provenance on this aircraft. Luckily, the folks at the Smithsonian employ such professionals.

It is a fact that Cole Palen of the Old Rhinebeck Aerodrome (New York) owned the Nieuport for many years before NASM acquired it. It flew in the summer weekend shows until retired to the Rhinebeck museum building in the late seventies. Despite a good number of false rumors about the airplane, including a suggestion that it was owned at one point by Howard Hughes, which was later dismissed by Smithsonian historians, the Nieuport 28 has clearly been put together with parts from several original aircraft and often repaired with nonoriginal parts.

What seems most verifiable is the fact that the serial numbers can be traced to late-production aircraft, which means the Nieuport 28 was not a war veteran. But at the same time, it was very likely a Hollywood star. (Or at least pieces of it were seen on the big screen.)

The NASM Nieuport 28 ended up in the hands of Paul Mantz. It seems that the aforementioned Garland-Lincoln sold all of their airplanes, including four original Nieuport 28s, to Paramount Pictures in 1938. From there all of the aircraft moved on to Mantz, who owned a company specializing in supplying aircraft for movie projects. Finally, Cole Palen traded a Standard J.1 to acquire the Nieuport 28, and it is believed that Palen likely pieced together many of the best Nieuport parts from the Mantz backlot.

Nieuport 28—Smithsonian, NASM

80

Curtiss MF Boat

Having grown up on a lake in upstate New York, Glenn Curtiss always understood the need for aircraft that could fly straight from the water. The US Navy saw this need as well, which is why Curtiss and the navy got along so famously. Flying from the water was a much more complicated task than rising from the ground. To start, the surface is not static, weather is exaggerated on water, and—perhaps the greatest challenge—the surface area between plane and water is much greater than that between ground and water, resulting in drag. Despite these obstacles, Glenn Curtiss had the patience and ambition to conceive of an aircraft that could reach the required speed by having the hull hydroplane on its step until the craft left the water for the air.

The Curtiss Model F came into use in 1913 and had a pusher configuration. Along with the US Navy, the Russian navy purchased the Model F for use along the Black and Baltic Seas. Before the Grigorovich M series flying boats, which truly represented the best of Russian flying-boat technology, the Curtiss M distinguished itself for a short time as one of its first aircraft stationed on the water in Russia. The years from 1913 to 1915 were important years for flying boats; many firsts were established during this brief period. Included in these achievements were

- the first aircraft to fly under automatic control using a gyroscopic stabilizer (designed by Elmer Sperry);
- the first aircraft to be launched by catapult from a warship while moving through the water (USS *North Carolina* in 1915); and
- the first US aircraft to see military action (launched from USS *Birmingham* in 1914 during the US occupation of Veracruz).

The Curtiss MF Boat, which stood for modified F Type, was a revised and improved version of the F and saw production begin in 1918. The US Naval Aircraft Factory was established in this same year in Philadelphia as an organized strategy to control the manufacture of necessary aircraft, now that the United States had entered the First World War. Keeping a factory of its own allowed the US government to understand pricing of aircraft versus the quantity pricing provided by private airplane builders. It also allowed for the development and testing of experimental aircraft should the need arise during the wartime effort. The main building where government aircraft were constructed is still around today at the Philadelphia Navy Shipyard.

The NAF was most concerned with the development of water-based patrol aircraft (flying boats) at first. Unrestricted German U-boat tactics were among the primary reasons the United States joined the war to end all wars. One of these designs was the Curtiss MF.

If you're visiting the Florida panhandle, the National Naval Aviation Museum (formerly the National Museum of Naval Aviation) in Pensacola is a worthwhile visit, as it is the home of the US Navy's Blue Angels. More relevant to our interests, it has some of the best examples of early flying boats in the world.

At the National Naval Aviation Museum, which was established in 1962 at the US Naval Air Station Pensacola, one can view the Curtiss MF boat. With serial number A-5483 and built at the National Aircraft Factory in 1918, this MF was one of the first deliveries of flying boats that came from the NAF. It saw US military duty until 1922, when it was purchased by a Massachusetts man and then sold again a year later to Italian pilot Eupilio Andreatto, who used it to tour the Northeast for demonstration flights.

Its last flight occurred in 1936, and then it was stored in a garage until acquired by George S. Waltman in 1960. The US Navy then purchased it and restored it in the same location where it was built, the original NAF site. It's been in Pensacola since 1968.

It seems that at least two other MFs exist. One, formerly in Cleveland as part of the Crawford Collection, is now in New Zealand as part of the Omaka Aviation Heritage Centre, which was purchased at auction in 2010 for the King Kong price of around $500,000. The other is on loan to the Curtiss Museum in Hammondsport, New York, from the Henry Ford Museum in Michigan.

Curtiss MF Boat—Pensacola

Benoist Tractor

[The State Historical Museum of Iowa in Des Moines, IA, USA]

Auto supply company owner Thomas Wesley Benoist anticipated the emergence of the aviation industry very early on. After only a year focusing on auto parts, he and his brother Charles switched gears to the aero parts supply trade. Called the Aeronautic Supply Company (a.k.a. Aerosco), in 1908 it was the first of its kind with a prospectus similar to a mini-Sears catalog. With fifty-two pages offering the sale of raw materials, engines, and aircraft themselves, Benoist and his company blazed a trail only five years after the Wright brothers first flew.

Despite his growing business, Thomas Benoist didn't fly in an airplane until 1910, when finally he took to the sky in a modified Curtiss pusher of his design. It is fair to say this solo flight mesmerized Benoist, and he was instantly hooked on flying. He flew often and became proficient enough to open a flying school. Besides the flying school and at least fifteen of his own aircraft designs, Thomas Benoist started the first commercial airline.

On January 1, 1914, a company called the Saint Petersburg-Tampa Airboat Line launched the first flight with an actual scheduled departure time. However, like many airlines today, the business was not profitable for Benoist. Larger aircraft design was needed, with passenger capacities of eight and more. This next step was never realized, however, as Benoist was killed in 1917 when he jumped awkwardly from a moving city trolley and died after hitting his head on a lamppost. He was only forty-three years old.

Among US states, Iowa's early aviation history is rather rich yet less reported than many other states (Texas, New York, Florida, etc.). An Iowa son, Oscar Solbrig was so taken with the Wright brothers' flights that he enrolled in the Glenn Curtiss Flying School in San Diego and later the Curtiss Flying Boat School in Hammondsport, New York. He became a respected exhibition flyer as his early career choice and started with a Curtiss-designed flying boat that he built himself. He later moved on to a Curtiss Headless pusher, half of which was built by the Curtiss Company, leaving the other half for Solbrig to complete to his own specifications.

Oscar Solbrig purchased an almost fully built Benoist tractor-configured airplane around 1916. He added an engine and flew it from time to time. As the United States moved quickly toward a war posture, Solbrig's exhibition flying waned, and he took to more lucrative ways of making a living. According to an article written by Robert Scheppler of Davenport, Iowa, that appeared in the *Aviation Historical Journal* in 1962, the following had been discussed with Mrs. Oscar Solbrig regarding her late husband's plane, now at the State Historical Museum of Iowa:

- It is an original Benoist aircraft with serial number 391.
- It may have cost approximately $400 when purchased.
- This Benoist was flown regularly until 1920 and stored until 1930.
- When pulled from the dust and reassembled, it was put on display at the Davenport City Museum, a former church.

Note: Legend has it that Mrs. Solbrig (Mary) was an expert mechanic.

As it turns out, the Davenport City Museum was razed in 1962, which led to a donation offer of the Solbrig Benoist to the Smithsonian. At that time, the Smithsonian lacked funding for even transporting the airplane, so other interested parties were pursued.

Louis Anderson of Mansfield, Missouri, stepped in and took temporary possession of the aircraft. The Solbrig family retained ownership, but Anderson restored the Benoist to some degree, and it was put on display at the National Antique Air Museum and Hall of Fame in Wichita, Kansas.

Finally, in 1968, the Benoist was donated by Solbrig family to the state of Iowa, where it can be seen hanging in the State Historical Museum of Iowa in Des Moines.

Benoist Tractor—The State Historical Mus.

Clark Ornithopter

[Owls Head Transportation Museum in Owls Head, ME, USA]

A compilation of original early aircraft would be incomplete if there were no listing of surviving known aircraft that attempted to fly but failed. In the very early days of flight, one of these categories, known as ornithopters, never had a chance to succeed.

Ornithopters are machines that attempt to emulate birds by flapping their wings mechanically so as to lift from the ground and achieve flight. We know now what was not known then; early twentieth-century technology would never find a method with the horsepower sufficient to lift a man and his machine by wing flapping. The Wrights, Langley, Chanute, etc. knew that the way to attain controllable, powered, sustained flight would likely be from copying the birds through observation of their glide. Despite this and what we now find obvious, there were some successes with wing-flapping vertical flight as early as the thirties. The German Alexander Lippisch built a craft that achieved flight by flapping its wings using efficient internal combustion engines.

Outside of the man-carrying attempts, there were many ornithopter successes as small toy or model designs. One such example is found today in the Smithsonian National Air and Space Museum. NASM maintains Victor Tatin's rubber-powered ortnithopter of the 1870s, which used an "active torsion" of the wings. This flew so well that a popular toy offered by Pichancourt using the Tatin design was sold in the 1890s. Other unmanned successes include the machine built by inventor Gustave Trouve, who used a gas engine to power his model in 1890, and those of Lawrence Hargrave who, in the 1880s, used rubber bands, steam, springs, and compressed air to achieve his model's lift abilities.

In any case, ornithopters were built in the late nineteenth and early twentieth centuries and, although (nonflying) works of art, very few survive today. The Owls Head Transportation Museum in Owls Head, Maine, is one of the few organizations to possess an original flying contraption.

The Owls Head Transportation Museum "is a nonprofit educational organization. Its mission is to collect, preserve, exhibit and operate pre-1940 aircraft, ground vehicles, engines and related technologies significant to the evolution of transportation for the purpose of education." The museum strives to keep things in operating condition, which is unique in today's static-display environment. Nevertheless, even the folks at Owls Head will not be able to make their Clark Ornithopter fly. But it will remain as a viewable piece of man's attempt to reach the clouds.

The Clark Ornithopter was built around 1900 by James W. Clark of Bridgewater, Pennsylvania. Clark was a clockmaker, inventor, and bicycle repairman who decided that flight was possible. He endeavored to construct a wooden biplane-configured craft that had wings designed to flap, powered by an engine. He covered the machine with turkey feathers (no longer part of the airplane display) and made several attempts to get her in the air. All attempts failed, and Clark moved on. However, the aircraft itself remained intact; it was stored in a carriage house and acquired around 1974 by Charles C. Lewis, a collector of toy soldiers, model boats, and aeronautica.

After Lewis's death, Christie's New York sold the ornithopter at auction in 1983, and it eventually made its way to Maine for display at Owls Head.

Of special interest in the construction of the Clark Ornithopter is the engine that was used in Clark's later test flights. The Waterman Motor Company, 5-horsepower, two-cylinder, vertical water-cooled engine was an early design of Cameron B. Waterman. A Yale graduate with a law degree, Waterman decided in 1905 that if a gas-powered engine could speed a motorcycle, then other uses were to be tested. Waterman became well known for developing outboard engines for small boats and formed the Waterman Marine Motor Company, which was sold in 1917 to the Arrow Motor and Marine Company of New York.

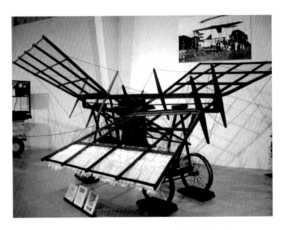

Clark Ornithopter—Owls Head

Nieuport 23 (Berliner Helicopter)

[College Park Aviation Museum in College Park, MD, USA]

Every once in a great while, we come upon an original early aircraft preserved today that is not only a rare bird in and of itself but also was used in experiments that contributed to aviation's advancement. The Berliner Helicopter is the perfect example.

Emile Berliner and his son Henry developed the first manned helicopter in the early twenties. Having purchased a war-surplus Nieuport 23 fuselage along with a 220-horsepower radial engine, the Berliners developed a mechanism that efficiently drove two wing-mounted counter-rotating propellers. These propellers faced up to the sky but could tilt slightly forward for yaw control. Pitch was controlled by a smaller tail-mounted propeller. In 1923 after testing, the Berliner helicopter received a third wing for safety, as it was thought that the plane, or rather gyrocopter, could glide to a landing if engine failure were to occur during flight.

The College Park Aviation Museum near the University of Maryland now displays the 1924 version of the Berliner Helicopter called the No. 5. It is owned by the Smithsonian Air and Space Museum and is appropriately on loan to the museum, as it was the College Park Airport where Henry Berliner conducted his test flights.

Ultimately, controllability was an issue for the Berliner Helicopter but not before it received great interest from the US Army Signal Corps. The US military continued testing the craft by moving it to McCook Field in Dayton, Ohio. Here, the Berliner achieved sustained heights of up to fifteen feet with forward speeds of forty miles per hour.

Experimentation in helicopter technology was certainly not monopolized by American inventors. As early as 1907 in France, successful but short flights were achieved using aircraft with vertical lift (not to be confused with an ornithopter's wing flapping, as discussed in an earlier chapter). Paul Cornu, a French bicycle maker, canceled all limitations of torque by combining counter-rotating rotors. Cornu used a small Antoinette engine and was able to lift about five feet off the ground; the aircraft remained stable for about a minute, an amazing feat, considering its weight.

The most famous name in helicopters, Igor Sikorsky, was fast at work on vertical flight in his native Kiev, Russia, in 1909 but had significant difficulty. His machine weighed four hundred pounds and could not rise off the ground with a passenger. This failure moved Sikorsky's interest away from helicopters until the thirties, when he returned to vertical flight experimentation and essentially created the helicopter as its own category of flight.

A few years later, around 1912 in Denmark, Jacob Ellehammer, famous later for various aircraft concepts, contributed a design with a stacked set of large counter-rotating rotors, twenty feet in diameter with six rotors, each five feet long, attached to the outside. These rotors would spin, producing vertical lift. It was a cumbersome aircraft but succeeded in making short hops.

Today, America's contribution, the Berliner Helicopter, sits in the middle of the College Park Aviation Museum. Opened in 1998 as an affiliate of the Smithsonian Institution, the museum contains twenty-seven thousand square feet of space and is located on the world's oldest continuously operating airport, College Park Airport. The airport was founded in 1909, when Wilbur Wright visited with the goal of giving flight lessons to the first American military aviators.

Nieuport 23 (Berliner Helicopter)—MD

Curtiss Seagull Flying Boat

[The Henry Ford in Dearborn, MI, USA]

The Henry Ford in Dearborn, Michigan, is an institution holding one of the world's best collections of, well, just about everything. One can find a Wright brothers bicycle just a few feet from the chair in which President Abraham Lincoln was assassinated. There are collections of sewing machines steps away from the Oscar Meyer Hot Dog car. There is the original (heavily restored) bus on which Rosa Parks was riding to work when she was arrested for refusing to give up her seat; this can be seen just around the corner from actual indoor locomotive engines that are two stories high. Outside the sprawling museum building, the collection continues in the form of a town called Greenfield Village, created specifically to illustrate the rare and unique set of Henry Ford's collection of famous buildings themselves. The original Wright brothers bicycle shop is found not in Dayton, Ohio, where a replica now stands but in Greenfield Village. It was taken brick by brick and reassembled in Dearborn.

Perhaps it goes without saying the transportation collection at the Henry Ford is extraordinary, with one of the best car collections in the world. Early aircraft survivors are well represented by a Blériot XI, a Curtiss JN-4C, and a Laird Biplane of 1915. Presently on loan to the Glenn H. Curtiss Museum in Hammondsport, New York are a Curtiss "Seagull" Flying Boat and a Standard J-1.

The Curtiss Seagull was the military version of the Curtiss MF Flying Boat. Though the Seagull was well constructed and quite beautiful, made of mahogany veneer with a pusher engine and fabric-covered wings, few were sold due to the overabundance of Curtiss MFs available as surplus after World War I. However, the Seagull was a reliable water-based aircraft even called romantic by some.

An interesting history follows the Seagull to its present location in Hammondsport. Although considered an unsubstantiated rumor, it is said that the Curtiss Seagull was a gift from Henry Ford to his mistress Evangeline Dahlinger. According to several Ford biographers, Henry Ford hired the capable mechanic and engineer Ray Dahlinger, who was loyal to Henry to a fault. It is said that Ford asked Ray to marry Evangeline so as to present a proper and respectable public appearance. Let's not forget that in the twenties, single women of a certain age were looked upon unfairly. Let's also not forget that Henry Ford was married and could not easily be seen with a single woman. A willing Evangeline did in fact marry a willing Ray Dahlinger and a secret relationship between Henry Ford and Evangeline could continue with little scrutiny.

According to biographer Stephanie Deutsch's *The Auto Didact: Inventing Ford's America*, Evangeline Cote was thirty years Ford's junior when she came to work as a stenographer. He arranged her marriage to his chauffeur, Ray Dahlinger; furnished a house; and later gave 150 acres of land to the couple. Deutsch notes that circumstantial evidence indicates that her son, John Cote Dahlinger, was Ford's child: "He provided his own baby crib for the child to sleep in, and when the boy was seven, he received a racing car from the Indianapolis 500, courtesy of Mr. Ford."

The Curtiss Seagull was presented to Evangeline Dahlinger as a gift from Henry Ford. She had become the first licensed pilot in Michigan. Ironically, the Seagull and other aircraft were later gifted back to the Henry Ford by Ray Dahlinger.

The Curtiss Seagulls were built from 1912 through the early 1920s. The Seagull in the Ford collection has been beautifully restored. The Seagull is a Model 18, which was the latest version of the design, built in 1919 with a 150-horsepower Hispano-Suiza engine.

As was the case with all early Curtiss aircraft, the names/designations of the aircraft were sometimes difficult to understand. They often changed after being redesignated. So in this example, the Curtiss Model MF Flying Boat is the modernized version of the original 1914 type; production started in 1918. The MF Flying Boat was later designated Model 18, as in The Henry Ford's example. The Seagull name was used for the postwar type, which had a seat for the pilot and one passenger as standard and was made available for civilians with the means to buy it. Some of the Seagulls had two additional seats and were designated as Model 25.

Standard J-1

If not for the Curtiss Jenny (JN-4D), the Standard Company's J-1 would likely have been voted America's most utilized aeroplane back in the late teens and twenties. Like Curtiss, Standard anticipated a need for aircraft as World War I began. This led to contracts with the US Army Signal Corp in 1916, the same year the Standard Aircraft Company became incorporated in Plainfield, New Jersey. The Sloane Airplane Company preceded Standard, and Charles Healy Day was the head aircraft designer for both firms.

Day has often been given the credit for designing aircraft propellers out of laminated wood. This gave the props much greater durability at a time when even taxiing an aircraft often led to small stones chipping the propeller before takeoff. The most famous of Day's designs, the Standard J-1, proved to be a bit of an unpopular trainer because it was initially underpowered, utilizing a Hall Scott engine. The underpowered engine had a reputation of providing an uncomfortable ride for both student and teacher, as the vibration was unnerving. Despite this, sixteen hundred were built by Standard and three other licensed manufacturers: Dayton-Wright, Wright-Martin, and Fisher Body.

Referring to the Standard J-1, Frank Tallman, the famous movie stunt pilot, remarked in his book *Flying the Old Planes*, "Stepping up for the first time to the massive wooden meat cleaver of a propeller on the front of the Standard would turn most any present-day mechanics' knees to jelly." But Tallman admits that he spent more time in a Standard J-1 than in any other aircraft and became fond of the plane. It may have rattled a bit and convinced its pilots that it would throw engine parts at any turn, but after hundreds of hours in the cockpit, Tallman, at least, knew the aircraft was trustworthy.

Like the Jenny, a good number of original Standard J-1s exist today, although most with the more powerful Hispano-Suiza engine installed. This is because in many cases the ineffective original motor was switched out after the war. Hispano-Suiza (which translates to "Spanish-Swiss") became a rather famous auto manufacturer after World War I. The Spanish-Swiss name refers to the partnership of a Spanish artillery captain, Emilio de la Cuadra, who was an automaker specializing in electric cars built in Barcelona, and the Swiss engineer Marc Birkigt, whose gasoline-powered engine design led the way.

Historical Aircraft Restoration's J-1 has an interesting history, having been on screen, as so many other World War I–era survivors have. Specifically, this Saint Louis–based original appeared in TV shows such as *The Fall Guy* and *The Young Indiana Jones*. Movie credits include *The Great Waldo Pepper*, *The Rocketeer*, and a brief showing in *Titanic*.

Ray Folsom, who had also owned and restored a Curtiss Jenny, acquired this J-1 and was the man who put it to work in Hollywood, beginning in the midseventies. The Historical Aircraft Restoration Museum acquired it around 2011, after Peck Aeroplane Restoration of Maryland Heights, Missouri, restored it back into its Waldo Pepper costume. It is housed in one of the museum's three hangars. But a trip to Creve Coeur Airport, which has both a grass field and a hard-surface runway, is well worth a visit, especially if you are a pilot and can fly in yourself.

Curtiss Pusher D

[Harold Warp Pioneer Village in Minden, NE, USA]

The next time you find yourself in the middle of Nebraska, it is highly recommended that you make a beeline for the rapidly aging museum known as the Harold Warp Pioneer Village. A little like a poor man's Henry Ford museum, the Pioneer Village was started with the same ambition as the Ford and even a good deal of money for the project.

Reminding one of the line in the movie *The Graduate*, when it is recommended to a young Dustin Hoffman that he pursue a career in plastics, Harold Warp did just that but at a far earlier time. According to historian Jim McKee of the *Journal Star*, "Harold graduated from high school and observed how chickens seemed healthier and laid eggs at a faster rate during the summer months. This he equated with sunlight and began experimenting with plastic coverings that would keep out cold winds yet allow the sun's warmth and ultraviolet rays to penetrate." This led Harold Warp to a successful business and eventually to great wealth with his product, Flex-O-Glass, in the late twenties.

Warp, a lifelong collector of Americana, founded his Pioneer Village in 1952 in Minden, Nebraska. Containing approximately fifty thousand items displayed in twenty-five buildings over twenty acres, the museum contains an original Pony Express station, a San Francisco cable car, and the first jet-fighter type, the P-59 Air Comet. Although the displays have grown old and lack the expensive daily care such a collection justifies, the items are nonetheless historically significant in many cases. With some ten aircraft (and many engines, propellers, etc.), the Pioneer Village possesses an original 1910 Curtiss Pusher, apparently flown by Charles Hamilton in the first New York-to-Philadelphia run. (Buyer beware: There isn't a great deal of provenance provided on the aircraft. There is little to indicate when exactly Warp purchased the plane and where he found it.)

The aircraft is suspended in the main museum building, sans original engine, which was said to have been removed after the Philly flight—this, the same engine used by Glenn Curtiss to win the 1909 Rheims race. If in fact this is the pusher that Hamilton used, it is a unique artifact. Charles Keeney Hamilton was known as the "crazy man of the air" because of his proclivity to perform risky loops, dives, and staged crashes.

Giving a new meaning to the term "DUI," a possible reason Hamilton was so willing to perform dangerous airborne maneuvers could be related to his often drunken state. One famous for imbibing, Hamilton was rescued more than once from crashes in which he was found to be completely intoxicated. Despite this, the Glenn Curtiss-trained pilot is forever remembered for being

- the first person to fly in the state of Washington;
- the first person to fly an aircraft in Tucson, Arizona;
- the first air visitor to Vancouver, Canada, from Tacoma, Washington (an international flight);
- the pilot to set a record for the quickest takeoff (seventy feet in 3.8 seconds); and of course
- the victor for being first to fly from New York to Philadelphia, which he did on June 13, 1910. The round trip took eleven hours.

Hamilton became a folk hero for some time and was rumored to have made as much as $250,000 with his exploits. What can be verified, however, is that he died in 1914 of tuberculosis and was penniless at that point. Piecing together the little that is known, it seems that Hamilton was making a cross-country tour starting in California and had damaged an aircraft or two on the way. Perhaps the Pioneer Village's Pusher is one of these, left unflyable.

Breese Penguin

[Cradle of Aviation Museum in Garden City, NY, USA]

Preparing an army rapidly is an integral goal of a country that finds itself in a world war. The United States, a late participant, had done its best to stay out of the war as hostilities raged in Europe. When the time came to reluctantly join the fray, training had to come together very quickly.

In the days before effective flight simulators, there was perhaps no better way to safely train air service personnel than to have them pilot a craft that acted in every way like a flyable aircraft but was unable to lift off the ground. The Breese Penguin was designed specifically to accomplish this.

With wings too short for flight, the Penguin demonstrated all the ground effects a pilot could expect just before takeoff and just after landing. The Penguin did not have brakes or wheels that could be controlled, as in a car. No, the pilot had to feel his way around the field just as if taxiing for flight and at nearly the same speed with the same lack of control.

The Cradle of Aviation Museum in Garden City, New York, boasts a fine collection of Long Island's aviation heritage. The Breese Penguin (1917) is the sole remaining example of a ground-only trainer that really represented, at least on paper, a way of saving money on repairs and perhaps pilots' lives during the ramp-up of a pilot's journey to soloing. Although three hundred were made, the idea was never a big hit, and formal training, using the Curtiss JN-4 (Jenny) and other actual flying machines was a process utilized far more often.

In any case both the Breese Penguin and its engine, the Lawrence 28 horsepower, were manufactured on New York's Long Island.

The aviation manufacturing industry on Long Island continued long after the Breese Company. Thirteen lunar modules (LMs) were built by Grumman, as well the navy F-14s, which were recently retired. Republic Aviation manufactured the P-47 fighter aircraft during World War II. And let's not forget that Amelia Earhart, Wiley Post, Roscoe Turner, and Howard Hughes started historic flights from Brooklyn's Floyd Bennett Field. And of course Charles Lindbergh began from Garden City's Roosevelt Field to capture the Orteig Prize for being the first to fly solo across the Atlantic Ocean.

The Cradle's Breese, often misspelled "Breeze," was purchased at the famous Christie's Wings & Wheels Auction held in 1982 and mentioned throughout these pages. Below is a list of the other early original aircraft sold at the W&W auction:

Built	*Aircraft*	*Present Location*
1917	Breese Penguin	Long Island, NY
1913–1918	Caudron G.3	Rio de Janeiro, Brazil
1917	Fokker DVII	Netherlands
1918	Pfalz DXII	Seattle, WA
1918	Morane Saulnier A1	Rhinebeck, NY
1917–1918	Curtiss JN-4D	Arkansas, then to Virginia
1912	Farman Shorthorn	Rockcliffe, Canada
1916	SPAD VII	San Diego, CA

- 1916   SPAD VII   London, UK
- 1918   Nieuport 28   Fort Rucker, AL
- 1918   Thomas Morse (S-4C)   Ithaca, NY
- 1912   Deperdussin Model C   San Diego, CA
- 1921   DH.4   Unknown
- 1917–1918 Sopwith Camel   Arkansas, then to New Zealand

Breese Penguin—Cradle of Aviation Museum

Blériot XI

New York's Long Island is situated like a giant runway jutting out into the Atlantic Ocean. It's no surprise, therefore, that its long history of aviation achievements has often had its takeoff from this part of New York State. Most famous of these was Lindbergh's historic Atlantic crossing in 1927, which began at Roosevelt Field in Garden City, Long Island.

But many years before Lindy's solo flight, Long Island was a well-appreciated and well-known magnet for America's earliest aviators. Joshua Stoff, the curator of the Cradle of Aviation Museum points out, "By 1909 the first daring flights were made from the Hempstead plains in the central part of Nassau County. Because the flat, open landscape made a natural airfield, famous aviator Glenn Curtiss brought his biplane, the Golden Flyer, here. By 1910 there were three airfields operating on the Hempstead Plains, and Long Islanders were building their own airplanes. Several flying schools and aircraft factories also sprang up, and Long Island became the center of the aviation world. By far the most important aeronautical event on Long Island up to this time was the 1910 International Aviation Meet at Belmont Park. The greatest aviators from all over America and Europe came to Long Island to show their latest flying machines, race, set records, and win prize money."

The Cradle of Aviation Museum, Long Island's renowned tribute to the area's skyward past, began when aviation superenthusiasts Kaiser and George Dade partnered with Henry Anholzer of Pan American Airlines and acquired various aircraft for restoration. We can't forget that Long Island was the home of such World War I aircraft manufacturers such as Sperry, LWF, Orenco, and Breese.

After the Kaiser and Dade group acquired its first airplane, a Curtiss JN-4D in 1973, the mission to establish a real brick-and-mortar museum began. In 1980, the former hangars of the Mitchell Air Force Base were utilized, while an aggressive expansion program led in 2002 to the beautiful Cradle of Aviation Museum that exists today. The Cradle's collection includes several original early aircraft, including the Curtiss Jenny, a Thomas Morse Scout ("Tommy"), a Blériot XI, and last chapter's Breese Penguin of 1918.

The Rhinebeck Aerodrome, just a couple of hours drive up the New York State Thruway, had for a long time three original Blériot XI's. Allowing other museums to share in Rhinebeck's Blériot riches, the Cradle of Aviation purchased Blériot number 153 through a donation of $100,000 from Alan Fortunoff, the well-known New York jewelry retailer.

This original Blériot was purchased by Rodman Wanamaker and has the distinction of being the first aircraft ever imported into America. It's important to remember that Wanamaker was a wealthy man with department stores in Philadelphia, New York, and Paris. Rodman Wanamaker had several hobbies, including golf, music, and aviation. It was Wanamaker who paid the Curtiss Company in 1913 to develop a flying boat that could cross the Atlantic Ocean. Out of this arrangement, the Curtiss America was developed but was never tested in crossing the oceans due to the outbreak of World War I.

Curtiss JN-4D

These pages document several Curtiss aircraft. This is simply because there are so many original early Curtiss types that survive today, especially the JN-4 (the Jenny), which has become an iconic example of a successful American early design. One cannot ignore the intriguing character of the man who was responsible for the JN-4D, the Curtiss Oriole, and countless other designs, Glenn H. Curtiss himself.

Glenn Curtiss introduced America to production flying boats, initiated at the request of the US military on the theory that aircraft with pontoons would be an effective tool for the US Navy. Curtiss's involvement with the US military would go on for many years and represented a stark difference to the approach taken by the Wright brothers, who were so guarded with their designs that they became reclusive.

As early as 1910, the Wrights were less enthused than Curtiss about the navy's attempts to develop aircraft for naval use. Even when it was decided that the first steps were to fly land-based aircraft off platforms on ships, the Wrights passed on the opportunity. The Curtiss Company, however, jumped at the chance, and on November 14, 1910, the Curtiss pilot Eugene Ely flew a Curtiss from a platform built on the bow of the USS *Birmingham*. This occurred at Hampton Roads, Virginia, an early base for Curtiss's navy exploits.

Such aggressive and opportunistic decisions by Glenn Curtiss were a staple of his personality. These traits were evident early in his life, perhaps as a result of his early experiences. Curtiss's father, Frank, who ran a harness business, died when Glenn was four years old. Financial necessities led to the end of Glenn's education in the eighth grade. He had to take a job and ended up at the Eastman Dry Plate Company, which was later to become Eastman Kodak. Being a natural engineer, he settled in Hammondsport, New York, with his young wife, seventeen-year-old Lena. Building and selling bicycles was his initial foray into a business of his own, but it wasn't long before Curtiss added engines to his cycles and eventually became a world-class motorcycle racer.

An interest in speed, fearlessness of danger, and great ambition led Glenn Curtiss to the budding aviation industry. Specifically, it was a visit by the balloonist Thomas Scott and Scott's request for a Curtiss-designed engine for his airship, called the *California Arrow*, that ultimately led to Curtiss's full-time interest in aviation.

Otto Kohl was an employee at the Curtiss Aeroplane & Motor Company in Hammondsport, where it must be noted that part of the landscape is the beautiful Keuka Lake, where Glenn Curtiss conducted many of his airboat experiments. Kohl had a lifelong interest in collecting Curtiss artifacts and had gathered enough to warrant a search for space. In the early sixties, a museum was dedicated.

Original Curtiss items including airplanes, motorcycles, and memorabilia were accumulated through the years, mostly through generous donations. In 1991, an appropriate location was established for the library, museum, and extended collection. Encompassing thirty-six thousand square feet, the Glenn H. Curtiss Museum has been particularly successful in building replicas of some of Glenn Curtiss's most famous aircraft. These include a replica of the 1908 June Bug, built by volunteers and then flown;

a full-size model of a Curtiss hydro-floatplane (also flown); and more recently, a full-size 1914 Curtiss Flying Boat *America*.

A featured original along with the original JN-4D is the Curtiss Oriole of 1919. It seems that both a Jenny and the Oriole serial number 853 were sold or perhaps donated to the Glenn Curtiss Museum around 1961 by Daniel and Floyd Hungerford. The Hungerford brothers were longtime aviation pioneers, having built a two-cylinder airplane engine as early as 1910. Dan Hungerford was Glenn Curtiss's mechanic for work on the flying boats.

The fuselage of the Oriole was used by the Hungerfords to test auto suspensions. This resulted in an aircraft with much damage and in need of repair, which it eventually received from the museum. The Oriole was a postwar design and therefore not a type listed on the survivor list in the compilation section of this book. However, according to a 2016 Wikipedia entry, besides the Hammondsport Oriole, "there is one on static display at the Minnesota Air National Guard Museum, an airframe in storage at the Fantasy of Flight Museum, Florida, and three in storage in East Wenatchee, Washington, at Century Aviation."

Thomas Morse Scout S-4B

[Ithaca Aviation Heritage Foundation in Ithaca, NY, USA]

Near the end of World War I, when the United States finally joined the fight, an advanced pursuit trainer was required. At a time when the Curtiss Jenny (JN-4) and the Standard J-1 were built as trainers but not universally popular, the Thomas-Morse S-4s rolled off the assembly line in Ithaca, New York. The year was 1918, and the "Tommy," as it was affectionately known, quickly became a pilot favorite. At a cost of about $5,400 each, a total of 460 were ordered, mostly for the US Army. A few went to the navy with floats.

William Thomas was born in Argentina but educated in England at the Central Technical College in London, earning a degree in civil and mechanical engineering. Thomas started experimenting with aircraft design in 1909, when he built his first plane, complete with a 22-horsepower auto engine.

William's brother Oliver joined him in aviation pursuits by forming both the Thomas Brothers Airplane Company, based in Ithaca, and the Thomas School of Aviation, New York State's first chartered air school. Prior to World War I, Thomas aircraft were highly regarded and therefore used to set many first flights in cities from San Juan, Puerto Rico, to Buffalo, New York. Once the war began, the Thomas Brothers Company merged with the Morse Chain Company to form the Thomas-Morse Aircraft Corporation. This is where the legend of the Tommy began, as production of the Thomas-Morse Scout quickly became arguably the most famous single-seat American aircraft of the First World War.

The Thomas-Morse Company, which essentially started production in Bath, New York, also built the S-4B during the war and prior to the first roll outs of the S-4Cs. Once the war ended, there were plenty of surplus Tommies in the United States. The Tommy now owned by the Ithaca Aviation Heritage Foundation (IAHF) was first thought to be the more common S-4C but later discovered to be an S-4B. With construction serial number 34544 (last military serial number A4358) USN, this aircraft was owned by a local San Diego resident and displayed in the San Diego Air and Space Museum in California for many years. The IAHF had been looking for an original Thomas-Morse SC-4 for some time, as they had a goal of bringing a Tommy back to its "birthplace." Their efforts were rewarded when Dr. William Thibault of San Diego made the very generous donation of a Tommy to be returned to Ithaca, where it was built.

In Ithaca there stands the same building on South Hill that produced the Thomas-Morse Scouts almost a hundred years ago. In fact, the woodworking machines used in the plant are still there and functional. When the stars align like this, one can only be compelled to restore the donated Tommy in the same place, with the same tools and with equal pride. But not all goes as planned in the world of aircraft restoration. The original Thomas-Morse factory had become the Emerson Power Transmission Company. But this is a story of a close community and generous neighbors, and Emerson ended up donating the equipment for the restoration, and a building was procured in Dryden, New York, through yet another donation, this time by Albert Height.

The IAHF Thomas-Morse Scout will be viewable at one point however, restoration participation as well as funding can be discussed through a visit to the website www.tommycomehome.org.

Nieuport 10

[Old Rhinebeck Aerodrome in Red Hook, NY, USA]

England has its Shuttleworth Collection, France has its Memorial Flight in La-Ferte Alais, and New Zealand has its Omaka Aviation Heritage Centre. In America, the Old Rhinebeck Aerodrome in upstate New York is one of the finest examples of an active old-time aerodrome in the world.

Started in 1951, the Old Rhinebeck Aerodrome (ORA) was conceived by Cole Palen, a.k.a. the Black Baron. Cole had the passion and foresight to understand that aging aircraft would eventually have value; Cole knew that one man's discarded surplus was another man's treasure, either as antiquities in a museum or as flying originals for the public to gather to see on summer weekends. So when it came time for Roosevelt Field on Long Island to close and make room for a shopping mall, Cole aggressively pursued the aircraft being sold and ended up with an original SPAD XIII, an Avro 504K, a Curtiss Jenny, a Standard J-1, an Aeromarine 39B, and a Sopwith Snipe. As was explained in Cole's 1993 obituary, "the story of how his new acquisitions were transported to upstate New York would make an epic tale in its own right. It took nine 200-mile round trips to move the aircraft back to the Palen family home where they were stored in abandoned chicken coops."

Palen later purchased a farm with a house near Rhinebeck, New York, and with income from his job as a mechanic for Texaco and the rental of his newly acquired aircraft for the film *Lafayette Escadrille*, the aerodrome thrived.

As is the custom with many of the finest museums in the world, the search to find what they feel may be missing from their collections is an on-going challenge, a challenge that becomes a great deal easier with open dialogue among respected organizations. Over the years, ORA has built a strong relationship with the Smithsonian National Air and Space Museum. In 1986 Palen arranged a trade of his Nieuport 28 for NASM's Nieuport 10, which now can be seen up on the hill in the newest of the ORA Museum buildings.

This particular Nieuport 10 was restored by the capable Old Rhinebeck Aerodrome restoration team back into the French ace Charles Nungesser's wartime theme. This was chosen because it is believed that this very plane was brought to the United States via Paris with stops in Cuba (exhibition shows) in 1924 by Charles himself. It was used for pilot training for a while and ended up at Roosevelt Field before being acquired by the Smithsonian NASM in 1951. Noteworthy here: the Nieuport 10 at Rhinebeck is really a modified aircraft built for training, called a Nieuport 83 E.2.

The Nieuport 10 was originally designed by Gustave Delage for participation in the 1914 Gordon Bennett Trophy race. This was canceled due to the start of the war, but the little biplane was developed as a two-seat reconnaissance aircraft that started to see service in 1915. Delage's design featured a V strut connecting a large wing above and a significantly smaller wing below. As time moved on, many of the aircraft were converted to single-seat planes that had the front seats covered; most received a Lewis gun.

Curtiss Model E

[Crawford Auto-Aviation Museum in Cleveland, OH, USA]

The Curtiss Model E was a 1910 hydroplane that was a bit bigger than the earlier land-based Curtiss Model D. The Model E was a "headless" aircraft, meaning it was without a front stabilizer and was an open biplane with both wings being of the same size. The land version had a tricycle landing gear, but the sea version utilized a large center pontoon with outrigger support floats. The headless-type Curtiss aircraft came about accidentally when it was noticed during a flying demonstration that the plane flew better without a front stabilizer. This discovery was made when a Curtiss pilot saw that his front stabilizer was broken and could not reattach it when attempting to put the plane together for its flight. In those days, planes were disassembled and reassembled often as they moved from town to town by train. The Model E became the first aircraft type to be purchased by the US Navy in 1911 at a mere $4,400 each. One of the fourteen that the navy purchased achieved the first catapult launch of a seaplane.

The Crawford Auto-Aviation Museum's Curtiss Model E, better known as the *Bumble Bee* (named by its first owner, Al Engel), is the only very early aircraft in the museum but a great example nonetheless. It was purchased by Engel for two reasons. He needed a new airplane, because his last one was apparently wrecked by making contact with a cow, and he wanted a plane that could land on water to avoid such field obstacles. As the story goes, Engel improved the engine and stretched the wings in order to take passengers on trips above Lake Erie. Paying customers allowed many a pilot in those days the financial assistance to stay aloft.

A native of Cleveland, Al J., as he was most often called, was a mason by trade and had the distinction of being a member of many flying clubs, including the Early Birds and Quiet Birdmen. Engel was also a veteran of the Spanish-American War and had learned to speak Spanish. This knowledge later assisted him in obtaining a position with the Curtiss Company training members of the Spanish air force on the latest Curtiss aircraft. Al J. founded the Engel Aircraft Company in Ohio to manufacture airplane parts and gliders for the army at the end of World War I.

After moving the Model E around the lakes of Northeastern Ohio, Engel decided to put the hydro in storage in 1914 in a garage in Cleveland. In 1946, he sold the aircraft to the Thompson Products Auto Album and Aviation Museum. Thompson Products was established by a forward-thinking Harvard man named Frederick C. Crawford. His company specialized in the manufacture and sale of metal fittings for the auto industry. Crawford decided that many an old car could be saved if he asked his sales team to keep their eyes open for opportunities. When an old yet valuable car was found, he purchased it through his company and began a museum. Eventually, the museum began to include airplanes. In 1964, the collection was merged with that of the Western Reserve Historical Society.

Today we think of Detroit as the hub of American transportation development, but it is the goal of the Western Reserve Historical Society to express to the public the important role Northeast Ohio played in America's transportation heritage. This includes boats and motorcycles as well. Museums these days don't typically restore artifacts the way the Crawford Museum does. In fact, they preserve in lieu of restoring, keeping the vehicles and artifacts in the near condition they were found in. The practices of the American Institute for Conservation of Historic and Artistic Works (AIC) are honored here. This means that any treatment undertaken by the museum to a vehicle must result in a similar appearance to its pretreatment condition and necessarily to a 'like-new' condition.

Packard Lepere LUSAC-11

[National Museum of the USAF in Dayton, OH, USA]

The US Army Signal Corps was unprepared for World War I, as evidenced by the lack of combat-ready aircraft. The total number of ready-to-fight US aircraft was zero.

By the time America entered the war, aviation had moved past the reconnaissance phase. At first, European combatants participated little in air combat. Other than the use of handguns from airplane to airplane and the occasional hand grenade, little weaponry was employed. (There was the story of a grappling hook dragged below a plane, however.) The first recorded aircraft brought down by another aircraft occurred in 1914 on the eastern front, when an Austrian aircraft on a reconnaissance mission rammed another aircraft, killing all occupants of both planes.

Machine guns attached to the front of a pusher aircraft was not a concept that was ignored. As early as 1912, the idea of an effective armed aircraft was on the drawing board at Vickers, but the flying performance of pushers made them obsolete, despite the optimal design for a front unobstructed machine gun configuration. It wasn't until October 1914 that a French pilot named Louis Quenault brought aboard a machine gun and proceeded to shoot at German airplanes effectively. From that time onward, machine guns became standard equipment and became exponentially more effective in shooting down enemy aircraft as they were incorporated into the design of new aircraft types.

Trainers were being built, and there was a mad dash to create a strategy to build American-made combat aircraft quickly. The plan was to have French-designed fighter planes built in the United States, and the LUSAC-11 was a prime example. It was a two-seat wood-and-fabric structure with a Lewis gun synchronized to shoot through the propeller. The observer's seat was surrounded by a "scarff ring" that effectively allowed a great deal of movement of the gun. The scarff ring was designed by Warrant Officer F. W. Scarff and employed a smart design that allowed for both swivel and elevation of the heavy gun with the use of a bungee cord and metal track.

Captain Georges Lepere of the French government, representing the French Aeronautical Mission to the United States, was asked to design the LUSAC-11 (Lepere United States Army Combat). The design was approved, and orders were placed with Fischer Body, Brewster & Company and Packard for 3,525 aircraft. Fortunately, the war ended, but unfortunately for the LUSAC manufacturers, the contracts were canceled. In all, only about twenty-five were produced. Although the LUSAC-11 never saw combat, it was used in altitude experiments, breaking the world record at 33,113 feet in 1920. At the controls was US pilot Major Rudolph William "Shorty" Schroeder. (He was six foot four.) The major broke the record but passed out at the controls. He regained consciousness as he approached the ground and survived the ordeal but suffered from diminished vision for the rest of his life.

The only surviving example of the Lepere LUSAC-11, viewable at the National Museum of the USAF in Dayton, Ohio, was formerly owned by one of the finest aviation museums in the world, the Musée de l'Air in Paris (Le Bourget Airport). Built at McCook Field, it was sent to France and possibly used for liaison services for US military attaches or as a test aircraft. The National Museum of the USAF acquired it in 1989, and it underwent a thorough restoration.

Caproni Ca.36

[National Museum of the US Air Force in Dayton, OH, USA]

War has a habit of accelerating technology. To think that in 1911 aircraft like the Antoinette VII represented the pinnacle of aviation advancement. Just a few years later, once World War I began, the need for observation, bomber, and fighter aircraft transformed the world of the flying machine into an environment of death from the sky.

The Italian engineer and businessman Gianni Caproni was a great believer in building large aircraft to transport people and supplies. He felt that if the aerodynamics and power source were correct, the size of the aircraft was unlimited. This concept was a leap in technological thinking and in most ways proved to be correct.

The Caproni Ca.3 epitomized the bigger-is-better concept and in 1916 showed the world that long-range bombing was possible. It should be noted that the Germans, Russians, and other powers built on similar philosophies for their own war strategies at around the same time. Such were the works of Zeppelin, Staaken, Gotha, Dornier, Flexistowe, and Sikorsky.

The Caproni Ca.3, of which there remain two survivors in the world today (Dayton and Vigna di Valle, Italy), was developed by repositioning the engine locations on the Ca.2. The first of the Ca.3s flew in 1916 and had three Isotta-Fraschini engines that together generated 450 horsepower. There was an engine placed on each wing and a pusher-configured third engine positioned midship behind the fuselage. The choice of engine for an aircraft this heavy was given much thought. Isotta-Fraschini was established as Fabbrica Automobili Isotta-Fraschini and known for the manufacture of luxury automobiles. Isotta-Fraschini produced its first aircraft engine, a water-cooled in-line four-cylinder, in 1910. When Caproni came calling, Isotta-Fraschini produced mostly six-cylinder engines, although the V.5 of 1915 was an inline eight. It turned out to be the right engine for the aircraft.

A crew of four—two gunners and two pilots—flew the large wooden biplane that had as its protection four Revelli 6.5 mm machine guns. The rear gunner manned upper machine guns while standing on the midplane engine inside what looked like a bird cage just in front of a propeller. Beneath the fuselage hung double main wheels under each engine and a tailskid at the end of each side of the lower wing. A heavy double nosewheel prevented damage and dangerous nose overs. (In Caproni designs after World War I, this nosewheel setup was removed, as nose overs became less likely.)

Of course the Ca.3 was a bomber, and it possessed a record rich in successful raids by war's end. Fifteen squadrons of the Italian Armed Forces were equipped with this type and bombed specific targets in Austria-Hungary, Libya, and some positions in France.

Today in Dayton, Ohio, at the National Museum of the US Air Force, an original Caproni Ca.36 is fully restored. The Ca.36 designation means that it is a slightly modified and later-built Ca.3. Marked with serial number 2378 but more likely with the actual serial number 25811 (found during the restoration), this Ca.36 was put out of service in 1934; it was then displayed in the Museo Caproni di Taliedo. When World War II began, the plane was disassembled and stored near Milan on Caproni family–owned land in an abandoned monastery, where it sat untouched for forty years.

Through negotiations between the Capronis and the National Museum of the US Air Force, it was decided in 1987 that the experts in Dayton would receive this rare antiquity and fully restore it for display in the United States on extended loan. It has been in the United States for nearly thirty years now.

Gianni Caproni was special and perhaps unusual in that he understood that preserving the historical heritage related to the development of Italian aviation was important for future generations. Because of this philosophy, the Caproni firm gathered an extensive collection of aircraft, related documents, and memorabilia. This led directly to the establishment of a private museum in which many of the finest examples of early aviation remain as survivors to this day.

Caproni Ca.36—Dayton

DH.4

Founded by the late Delford M. Smith, the Evergreen Aviation and Space Museum in McMinnville, Oregon, started as a collection of vintage aircraft inspired by Smith's son, Captain Michael King Smith. After the tragic automobile accident that took Captain Smith's life in 1995, his father proceeded to build the collection into what he and his son had long envisioned.

Well established in aviation for decades, the Evergreen companies in Oregon include entities such as an airline and a helicopter services. On the nonprofit side, the aircraft collection is housed in a beautiful museum that boasts a variety of both military and civil craft. The grounds provide many attractions for visitors, including a waterpark, but it is a very large artifact that gets the most attention.

Howard Hughes's Hercules H-4, better known as the *Spruce Goose*, is part of this fine collection, and despite its size, it fits comfortably in a glass hangar. Hughes took on the task of building a troop transport to ferry soldiers across the Atlantic during World War II—a reasonable undertaking until one realizes that Hughes was restricted to an all-wood design because of the necessity of conserving metal at the time. Through great cost and many difficulties, the birch (not spruce) aircraft was completed and flown only once and very briefly on November 2, 1947, long after the war ended. The Hercules is the largest flying boat ever built and has the largest wingspan of any aircraft in history. The Smiths purchased the plane for $500,000 from the Aero Club of Southern California, where it was previously viewable beside the Queen Mary in Long Beach.

While there are few original aircraft from the era of our interests at the museum, there is an impressive set of World War I replicas, including a Sopwith Camel, a Nieuport 11 "bebe," and a Fokker Dr.1 Triplane (of which no original examples survive today).

But those seeking to see a documented early original will not be disappointed, as there is a gem within these halls. A De Havilland DH.4M, built in 1918 with civilian serial number N3258, is on display. Stewart W. Bailey, the curator, explains that the DH.4, recently valued at $1.3 million, "was originally built under license from de Havilland circa 1918 by the Fisher Body Division of General Motors. Later, in 1923, this plane was one of 180 DH.4s modernized by the Boeing Aircraft Company in Seattle, Washington. Converted for mail hauling, the new DH.4M-1 was assigned the civil registration number 3258. After being passed through a series of civilian owners, the plane was sold in 1937 to Paramount Pictures. It appeared in the 1938 movie *Men with Wings*. Famous movie pilot Paul Mantz flew stunts for the movie, and in 1941, he purchased the aircraft from Paramount. The plane also appeared in the films *The Court-Martial of Billy Mitchell* (1955) and *The Spirit of Saint Louis* (1957). In 1962, Mantz lent the DH.4 to the US Marine Corps to use as a pattern to construct a museum replica. Mantz was killed while filming the final flight scenes of the movie *Flight of the Phoenix* (1966), and the DH.4 was sold at auction the same year."

The DH.4 was purchased by Evergreen in 1990 after it had been displayed in many different museums over the years. Throughout the nineties visitors to Seattle's Museum of Flight could see the rare aircraft on loan from Evergreen. Upon its return to

Oregon and the opening of Evergreen's new museum building in 2001, the DH.4 moved comfortably back in, sharing space with such aviation icons as a Boeing B-17, a P-51 Mustang, and a P-38 Lightning that are also a part of Evergreen's impressive collection.

As of this writing the Evergreen Aviation and Space Museum has undergone some collection changes, and in 2015, the ownership of the aircraft transferred to the Collings Foundation of Stow, Massachusetts. It will, however, continue to be displayed at Evergreen for an undetermined amount of time.

DH.4—Evergreen Aviation and Space Museum

Wright Flyer (B)

[The Franklin Institute in Philadelphia, PA, USA]

Philadelphia, the first capital of the United States, prides itself on its role as one of America's heritage cities. And as would be expected, its museums proudly demonstrate this, perhaps none better than the Franklin Institute. Named after its founder, Benjamin Franklin, the Institute was founded in 1824 and is therefore the oldest center of science education and development in the United States.

With a reputation for making important strides in the development of steam engines and the study of water power, the Franklin Institute of Pennsylvania for the Promotion of the Mechanic Arts, as it was originally called, was established to recognize scientific advancements. Not surprisingly, an original early Wright aircraft is part of the collection. The Wright Flyer Model B, purchased new by Grover Bergdoll in 1912, has the distinction of being one of only two in the world today. (The other is in the National Museum of the USAF in Dayton, Ohio.) There is an original Wright Model A in Munich and a 1905 Wright Flyer III in Dayton at the Carillon Historical Park.

It was 1909 when the Wrights finally decided to build a manufacturing concern after so many years of hiding their invention from the world. Clearly competent businessmen, they set up a factory in their hometown of Dayton, Ohio; a training school at Huffman Prairie, Ohio; and corporate headquarters in New York. The Wrights were happy with the headless configuration and successful testing of the Model B, and the first Wright production aircraft was made available. William Burgess produced many of what he called the Model F, which had the distinction of being the first aircraft produced under license in the United States. The Burgess Company and Curtis, Inc., founded in 1910, and known for shipbuilding in Massachusetts, set out to build aircraft at the very dawn of the industry. Ironically, the name Curtis refers not to the Wright brothers' enemy, Glenn Curtiss, but to Burgess's partner, Greely Curtis. Even more ironic is the fact that in 1914, the Burgess Company would be sold to the Curtiss Aeroplane and Motor Company.

This first license arrangement was well negotiated by the Wrights, as they received licensing fees of one thousand dollars per aircraft and one hundred dollars per exhibition flight. The contract also required the Burgess design to be exactly like that of the Wright Model B to the letter. This fact was promptly ignored by Burgess, and his company built aircraft with pontoons for water landings, a move that in part led to the end of the license contract. In any case, the days of a Wright-designed aircraft needing a catapult and track for launch were now gone.

With Wright production aircraft available to the general public, the Wright brothers' products would be seen far and wide. However, the Wrights, known for being stringent and organized micromanagers of their brand name, insisted that all those purchasing one of their aircraft must come to Dayton to take flying lessons at their factory. Once abilities were seen in potential pilots, the proud owners could have their aircraft, for which they paid $5,000 apiece.

Philadelphia native Grover Cleveland Bergdoll was willing to participate in this ritual and received his newly built Wright Model B in 1912. Bergdoll, far from a hobbyist, made the most of his new purchase. He flew his Wright plane a documented 748 times without a major problem. His longest flight was a two-and-a-half-hour journey and covered 110 miles. Altogether, his Wright Model B, which is now on display at the Franklin Institute, logged 312 hours in the air before being retired, an amazing feat for an aircraft built in 1912.

With serial number 39, Bergdoll's Wright plane was stored in his workshop in Pennsylvania from 1914 until 1933 and, unfortunately, was likely vandalized, as it was missing the engine, radiator, and control stick. Before Bergdoll donated the plane to the Franklin Institute in 1935, he, with the help of the Camden County Vocational School in Merchantville, New Jersey, restored the plane to flyable condition. It flew to commemorate the Wrights' first flight on December 17, 1934.

Curtiss JN-4D

Glenn Hammond Curtiss has been called the father of the American aviation industry. Like the Wright brothers, Curtiss started with bicycles. He was most famous for racing bicycles until he moved on to competitive motorcycle racing. Today, a Curtiss-manufactured motorcycle is rare and in some cases brings a six-figure auction price. Unsatisfied with anything short of the latest engineering technology, Glenn Curtiss began to build engines for early airships in 1904. While working with Alexander Graham Bell, who had an interest in aviation as well, Curtiss formed the Aerial Experiment Association, known better by its acronym AEA. In 1908, this unique group endeavored to build machines that flew. Besides unprecedented advances in seaplane technology working with the US Navy, Glenn Curtiss also accomplished

- a win at the first international air races in France;
- the first publicly witnessed sustained powered flight; and
- the first long-distance flight in the United States (Albany to New York City with two stops).

The Curtiss Jenny owned by the Flying Heritage Museum in Seattle may be the best flying example of a Jenny in the world. This is quite a distinction, considering that far more Curtiss Jennies (JN-4D and JN-4C; Canuck) have survived than any other original early aircraft type—perhaps fifty examples. Let's also remember that there were more than six thousand Jennies built during World War I, a very high number relative to other aircraft types of the era.

Robert Casari, author of *Encyclopedia of US Military Aircraft, The World War I Production Program, Vol. 3, The Curtiss Jennies*, has suggested Jenny number 3712 was one of 252 built in May 1918 at Curtiss. It was stationed at March Field near Riverside, California, as a training aircraft for US Army flying cadets. Although its service history is unknown, it seems that the Jenny was sold back to the Curtiss Company in 1919 and refurbished. Licensing paperwork reveals that the airplane was purchased from Howard Williams in 1925 by Earl Kampschmidt of Los Angeles and his partners. The Flying Heritage Museum's (FHM) Jenny (3712) was then apparently flown often, which led to crashes and other incidents that resulted in the aircraft being declared "very bad and old" by an aviation inspector.

After several years and various owners who were the partners of Kampschmidt, number 3712, which was assigned the civilian serial number NC2939, was sold a few more times before ending up with Ray Folsom of Hermosa Beach, California, in the midseventies. Any early aviation fan has certainly seen *The Great Waldo Pepper*. The aircraft used in the film was another Ray Folsom–owned antique, a Standard J-1, which is similar in appearance to a Jenny. It was in 1998 that FHM purchased the Jenny from Folsom but in nonflying condition. This was remedied once that aircraft was sent to Texas for a full restoration by Vintage Aviation, a highly regarded company based in Kingsbury, specializing in work on such early original examples.

The provenance of Jenny 3712 is well documented, thanks to the efforts of military aviation curator Cory Graff, who has shared his research with the public. The Flying Heritage Museum was founded in 1998 by Microsoft founder and modern philanthropist Paul Allen. Having a lifetime passion for aviation and history in general, Allen has the planes in his collection fully restored to flying condition. This is accomplished with exacting detail and a focus on authenticity, despite the costs involved. Although the FHM Collection is focused on the World War II aircraft of several countries, the Jenny is superb in every way and represents the start of America's aviation heritage. The collection is operated by Friends of Flying Heritage, an organization that has a strong focus on education. When not working on various business projects under the Vulcan name, Allen owns the Seattle Seahawks of the National Football League (NFL), the Seattle Sounders of Major League Soccer (MLS), and the Portland Trail Blazers of the National Basketball Association (NBA).

Caproni Ca.20

In wartime, not all participants are combatants; in World War I, airplanes themselves were not expected to fight at first. However, the Caproni Ca.20 is an exception and was designed for air combat as perhaps the first true fighter plane. The presence of a Lewis .303-caliber machine gun perched on supports above the pilot's head and just out of reach of the propeller left no doubt about this aircraft's intent. In 1914, this design was ahead of its time; it was thought that aeroplanes had only certain functions such as reconnaissance, patrol, and facilitation of communication. Armed engagement with the enemy was not expected, and therefore, few designs anticipated such barbaric activity. In fact, not even Caproni, the manufacturer, was thinking in terms of dogfights or ground-strafing missions. This is clear from the fact that only one Ca.20 was ever built. Societa de Agostini e Caproni (later renamed Societa Caproni e Comitti) chose instead to focus on heavy bombers, as these were thought to be the future of warplanes.

Giovanni Battista Caproni was Italy's finest young aeronautical engineer by 1914, when war broke out. He began his career in aviation in 1907 by building aircraft engines at a time when motorcycle engines were still being used in aircraft. Although the Caproni Ca.20 was a small, light, one-man monoplane, Gianni Caproni as he was known, became a celebrated builder of large aircraft. From multiengine biplanes to colossal triplanes, he courageously designed aircraft that simply looked too big to be safe. In fact, many crashed, including an airliner he created called the Ca.48 that was involved in the first airline disaster in 1919. Based on conflicting reports, between fifteen and seventeen people were killed near Verona, Italy.

Through an acquisition from the Caproni family in Trento, Italy, where the Gianni Caproni Aviation Museum is housed, the Museum of Flight added this rare aircraft to its already impressive collection. The museum's collection covers all eras, with an emphasis on the US Northwest's aviation history. The museum, which was started in 1964 by the Pacific Northwest Aviation Foundation, is not shy about its interest in Boeing, as both organizations share the same grounds. The Red Barn, which is the actual building in which Boeing started, is now part of the museum and was shipped by barge to its present location. Some of the stars of the collection, such as the Aviatik DI and a Pfalz DXII, both 1918 originals, and several World War II aircraft were acquired by the museum from the Champlin Fighter Museum in Mesa, Arizona. The Champlin closed in 2003 after being open to the public for twenty-two years.

The Caproni family kept many of Gianni's original aircraft just as he had left them. The Ca.20 is no exception. It still wears its original fabric and remains untouched after eighty-five years of storage. There also exists an original Ca.22, Gianni Caproni's 1913 model designed for better pilot visibility. It now resides far from Europe in New Zealand as part of the increasingly significant Omaka collection.

Caproni Ca.20—Museum of Flight

Boeing Model 6 (B-1)

Washington State, still known today as a primary US source for timber, was at the turn of the century a frontier ripe for spruce harvesting. Weyerhaeuser is still one of the top five employers in Seattle today.

It is Seattle where the young Detroit native William Boeing moved with an eye on building his fortune in the lumber trade. Having enjoyed a privileged childhood as the son of a German-born mining engineer, William attended Yale. In 1903, he decided to move to the Pacific Northwest and purchase land in the frontier of Washington State. He purchased interests in lumber companies in an area known as the Olympic Peninsula, which is just across Puget Sound from Seattle. The peninsula was unmapped until 1900 and consists of thirty-six hundred square miles of land.

As president of Greenwood Timber Company and with an interest in building wooden boats, William Boeing laid eyes on an airplane for the first time in 1909 at the Alaska-Yukon-Pacific Exposition. He quickly saw the potential of aircraft, specifically wooden aircraft that could land and take off from the water.

In 1916, Boeing founded the Pacific Aero Products Company in Seattle with partner George Westervelt, a navy engineer. Westervelt and Boeing designed and built the B&W seaplane, the company's first aircraft. As the United States entered the Great War, Boeing developed a production aircraft called the Model C. Around this same time, Westervelt was called back to duty, as US participation in the war ramped up. William Boeing changed the name of his company due to Westervelt's exit, and on May 9, 1917, the Boeing Airplane Company was born.

The Models Cs were seaplanes, well timed for navy air service, and more than fifty were sold to the US Navy, based in Pensacola, Florida. Used successfully as a trainer, the Model C established Boeing in this new industry. In 1919 the Boeing Model 6 (B-1) was designed and built. The Model 6 (B-1) flying boat was Boeing's first nonmilitary design. The pilot sat out in front with the pusher Hall-Scott engine behind. The aircraft had two open cockpits, with the pilot in the front section. Ultimately, only one was ever built, despite Boeing's burgeoning reputation, as there were simply too many surplus aircraft available after the war. The aircraft manufacturing industry plummeted. Boeing only survived by diversifying its manufacturing choices, offering furniture and wooden boats.

Also known as MOHAI, this Seattle museum is the largest heritage museum in the state of Washington, with annual attendance of sixty thousand. With four million artifacts, the museum focuses on education for the people of the Pacific Northwest. The one and only B-1 was used to deliver mail to remote areas north of Seattle by Edward Hubbard, who bought the plane in 1920. The Seattle Museum of History and Industry received the Model 6 (B-1) in 1954. It had been well kept after it was retired in 1930.

When one thinks of Seattle, Boeing may be the first company that comes to mind (except perhaps Microsoft or Starbucks). Despite having corporate offices in Chicago, however, Boeing still employs seventy thousand people in Seattle. Worldwide, Boeing employees are working in sixty-five countries. It is ironic that the Boeing Company started with small seaplanes; this same company would establish itself forever in military history for designing and building the workhorse heavy bomber B-17 and the eventual war-ending B-29 that carried the atomic bomb in World War II.

Boeing Model 6 (B-1)—Seattle

The Homebuilts

In the beginning there were the Wright brothers; Glenn Curtiss; and various French entrepreneurs such as Louis Blériot, Maurice Farman, Gabriel Voisin, and the Caudron brothers, Gaston and Rene. These and other respected businessmen were the local inventors who contributed to aviation's history in conspicuous fashion. These were the men (and women) who often borrowed from successful designs but created their own aircraft to satisfy a need to put their own indelible marks on an industry in its infancy or, frankly, due to a lack of funds. While one could purchase a Blériot XI or the American-made Benoist, it was simply cheaper to copy one.

In those early years, it was understood that brand-name aircraft were not affordable for all. This is when mail-order aeroplane parts providers began to spring up and offer catalogs for the do-it-yourselfer. In contrast to the Wright brothers, who were very guarded about their aviation design contributions, the spirit of the day and an interest in aviation's advancement led even famous aviators such as Alberto Santos-Dumont to offer design drawings of their aircraft. The construction of the Santos-Dumont Demoiselle was published in the June 1910 edition of *Popular Mechanics*.

Today, one can see quite a few original homebuilts from the early 1900s, including

- **1915 McCabe Baby**, displayed at the Dawson County Historical Museum in Lexington, Nebraska;
- **Nixon Homebuilt**, found at the New England Air Museum in Windsor Locks, Connecticut;
- **1915 Laird Biplane**, at The Henry Ford in Dearborn, Michigan;
- **1916 Ingram Foster Biplane**, displayed at the Albuquerque International Airport, Sunport, New Mexico;
- **1911 Pliska Aeroplane**, viewable at the Midland International Airport in Midland, Texas;
- **1910 Maupin Lanteri Black Diamond**, owned by NASM but displayed at the Hiller Aviation Museum in San Carlos, California;
- **1912 Montgomery Evergreen**, owned by NASM but displayed at the San Diego Air and Space Museum in San Diego, California;
- **1911 Steco (Stephens Co.)**, now at the National Motorcycle Museum in Anamosa, Iowa;
- **1910 Hartman Monoplane**, at the Harold Warp Pioneer Village in Minden, Nebraska;
- **1910 Von Palmer Biplane**, on display at the Empire State Aerosciences Museum in Scotia, New York;
- **1912 Bates Tractor**, at the EAA Airventure Museum in Oshkosh, Wisconsin;
- **1911 Baldwin Red Devil**, at the Smithsonian NASM in Washington, DC;
- **1912 Fowler Gage Biplane**, at the Smithsonian NASM in Washington, DC; and
- **1913 Ecker Flying Boat**, at the Smithsonian NASM in Washington, DC.

Gonzales No. 1 Biplane Tractor

The sibling threesome of Gonzaleses (Arthur, Willy, and Eddie), residing in San Francisco in the early 1900s were prime examples of the spirit of early aircraft ingenuity. Their Gonzales No. 1 Biplane Tractor was one of two creations built from scratch by the Gonzaleses around 1910. It's hard to imagine climbing aboard an aeroplane built in one's own backyard out of spruce and bicycle parts with the design coming from photos of other flying machines, but that's just what the eldest brother, Eddie, did. Despite having no education past the third grade, the Gonzaleses eyed the prize of sustained flight and the prospect of selling their invention. When word got around that a Kemp engine, rather than an Anzani, would successfully power the aircraft, the Gonzaleses were on their way. In fact, the Wright brothers made a visit to the west to see the Gonzales No. 1, in case there were patent infringements. No wing warping here!

While the plane flew from dune to dune in the Richmond district of San Francisco, the hope of a financial boon through the manufacture and sale of the airplane was never realized. There is no record of any of the airplanes being sold. With a family move to Los Angeles in 1915, the biplane ended up in the basement of the boys' aunt. Finally, in 1975, Bob Gonzales, the grandnephew of the Gonzales aviators, retrieved the biplane and put it on display at Travis AFB, where some restoration work was conducted. It was later loaned to the Hiller Air Museum in San Carlos, California, before coming to rest at the Nut Tree Center for Patriotism in Vacaville, California.

Laird Biplane

As discussed in these pages, The Henry Ford in Dearborn, Michigan, is one of the most interesting museums in the United States. It is an amalgamation of items collected through the decades that started as Henry Ford's own collection of household items that he felt revealed true American innovation. The Henry Ford (the museum, not the person) has acquired items large and small and preserved them in a space big enough to accommodate Yankee Stadium. (One wonders why the original Yankee Stadium isn't part of the collection today; after all, the original Logan County, Illinois, courthouse where Abraham Lincoln practiced law is there, having been moved to Dearborn.)

The Laird biplane donated to tThe Henry Ford by Emil Matthew Laird in 1936 was built by Laird in 1915. He was from Chicago, Illinois but later moved to Wichita, Kansas, where he began his manufacturing endeavors. It is a one-of-a-kind biplane made of fabric and wood (spruce), utilizing the Anzani motorcycle engine that was very popular among early aircraft inventors. Although Emil Laird was only seventeen, he successfully built and flew this plane. It was also flown by Katherine Stinson, who was known as the "Flying School Girl," due to her youthful appearance. Stinson was the fourth woman to obtain a pilot's license in the United States. She took this particular airplane to Asia to demonstrate her ability to "fly like the boys."

Emil Laird later became known as the first commercial aircraft manufacturer by creating the "Swallow" in the early twenties. He was also a highly respected air racer, partnering with Roscoe Turner in the late thirties.

Ingram Foster Biplane

The Pioneer Aeroplane Exhibition Company was started by two Texans, Jay Ingram and Charles Foster. Ingram, who owned an early Ford dealership in 1914 in Decatur, Texas, was a good match for his partner, Foster, who was a professional exhibition flier. Although their company didn't enjoy a long and prosperous business run, several planes were built from scratch, copied directly from a Curtiss Type Pusher. The parts were purchased through catalogs or custom built from materials found in local lumber yards.

Most interesting about this homebuilt plane was the method by which it was preserved. Because it was built to be used as an exhibition plane and viewable across the Southwest, crates were built to keep the biplane safe and intact for shipping via railroad; tools were crated, also. The rail system was used because flying the plane itself would entail too many fuel stops. The crates were so sturdy that once the Exhibition Company had closed shop, the biplane stayed crated, well preserved for seventy years.

In 1968, a Lampasas, Texas, pilot and restorer purchased the Ingram Foster from the Ingram family and pieced it back together. In 1987, the city of Albuquerque bought the airplane, as it represented an original of the Curtiss type Charles Walsh flew at the 1911 New Mexico Territorial Fair. This was New Mexico's first aeroplane flight.

The Ingram Foster Biplane can now be seen at the Albuquerque International Airport (Sunport) in New Mexico.

Pliska Aeroplane

John Pliska, an immigrant from Austria and then a citizen of the Unites States of America (he was the first naturalized citizen in Midland County, Texas), was a skilled blacksmith. Having been fascinated with aircraft since his days in the Austrian balloon service, he set out to build his own craft in 1911.

Pliska, with the help of Gray Coggin, an auto mechanic, built a plane using only wire, wood, and unvarnished cloth. The plane they built could fly, although in short hops. It was a copied design taken from the Wright Flyer II, which Pliska studied closely when Robert Fowler, a renowned pilot and show flyer, toured Midland. Over time, the Pliska was modified to protect it from wear and tear during the short test flights, and eventually the aircraft was stored at Pliska's blacksmith shop. There it stayed until the early sixties, when members of the Pliska family donated the plane to the city of Midland, where it can be seen today at the Midland International Airport.

Bates Tractor

Carl S. Bates of Clear Lake, Iowa, was an avid aeronaut whose interest in aviation began while he was a teenager in the late 1890s. He attended the prestigious Armour Institute of Technology in Chicago, where Octave Chanute was a professor. Having learned a great deal about aeronautics and the relationship between weight and lift, Bates set out to build his own flying machine.

In addition to his powered aircraft, he built hang gliders and improved the design, which he wrote about in magazines of the day. After emulating and building Curtiss-type biplanes, he settled in 1911 on a monoplane design that can be seen today in the EAA Airventure Museum in Oshkosh, Wisconsin.

Part Two: Collections Compilation

ANTARCTICA

Mawson's Huts Foundation

Cape Denison, Commonwealth Bay
ANTARCTICA

Type	Year	Serial number	Notes
Vickers REP	1911		• Remains of Mawson's aircraft used unsuccessfully in flight and as a method of towing equipment on the ice. • Discovered by Australian search team; metal wreckage exposed in melting ice. • Not viewable and likely in the ocean by now.

Mamson's Vickers REP

AFRICA

Ditsong National Museum of Military History

Erlswold Way, Saxonwold (Johannesburg)
SOUTH AFRICA

www.ditsong.org.za/militaryhistory.htm

Type	Year	Serial number	Notes
Airco DH.9		2005	• Marked I.S8.
RAF SE5a	1917	F7781/3	• Marked A.24.

ASIA

Junagarh Fort

Junagarh Fort Road
Bikaner, Rajasthan 334001
INDIA

www.junagarh.org/history.html

Type	Year	Serial number	Notes
DH.9	1918		• Two other dilapidated DH.9s were purchased. • One remains in India.

DH.9 at Junagarh Fort

126

Kakamigahara Aerospace Science Museum

5–1 Shimogiri-cho
Kakamigahara 504-0924
JAPAN

www.city.kakamigahara.lg.jp/museum

Type	Year	Serial number	Notes
Salmson 2A-2	1922		• Similar to those built at Kawasaki shipyard.

Iruma Air Base

Educational hangar for JASDF called Shubudai Memorial Hall.

Sayama, Saitama
JAPAN

Type	Year	Serial number	Notes
Henry Farman III	1922		• Apparently restored at Dayton. • Japan's first airplane. • Wheels and engine are all that is original.

Henry Farman III at Iruma Air Base

Istanbul Aviation Museum

Military Airport
İstanbul-Yeşilköy
TURKEY

www.hho.edu.tr/muze/muze.htm

Type	Year	Serial number	Notes
Grigorovich M-5	1915	"31"	• Russian naval example that made an emergency landing in Turkey.

AUSTRALIA

Smith Brothers Memorial

Vimy Walk
Adelaide Airport, 5950
AUSTRALIA

www.monumentaustralia.org.au/themes/people/aviation/display/50123-ross-and-keith-smith

Type	Year	Serial number	Notes
Vickers Vimy	1919	F8630	• Restored, London-Darwin flight.

Australian War Memorial

Treloar Crescent
Campbell ACT 2612, Canberra
AUSTRALIA

www.awm.gov.au

Type	Year	Serial number	Notes
Airco DH.9	1918	F1287	• Acquired by the museum in 1922.
Albatros DVA	1917	D5390/17	• Forced down and captured, Dec. 1917.
Avro 504K		H2174	• Was on loan to Qantas Airlines.
Pfalz D.XII	1918	2600/18	• Given to Australia as part of Armistice agreement.
RAF SE5a	1918	C9539	
Deperdussin	1912	CFS.5	• Oldest existing Australian military aircraft.

Harry Butler Memorial

Maitland Rd
Minlaton SA 5575
AUSTRALIA

www.captainharrybutler.com

Type	Year	Serial number	Notes
Bristol M1C Monoplane	1918	C5001	• Sole surviving example of "Puck." • Known as "The Red Devil"; used by Harry Butler to deliver mail from Adelaide to Minlaton in 1919.

Bristol M1C at Harry Butler Memorial

The Australian National Aviation Museum

CNR First Street and Second Avenue
Moorabbin Airport
Melbourne 3194
AUSTRALIA

www.aarg.com.au

Type	Year	Serial number	Notes
RAF BE2a	1913		• Wings only, rare NPL3a aerofoil (Andrew Willox).

Yarrawonga-Mulwala Pioneer Museum

151 Melbourne Street
Mulwala NSW 2647
AUSTRALIA

www.mgnsw.org.au

Type	Year	Serial number	Notes
Sloane Biplane	1913		• Details featured in an earlier chapter of this book.

Royal Australian AF Museum

RAAF Base Williams
Point Cook Road
Point Cook, Victoria
AUSTRALIA

www.airforce.gov.au/raafmuseum

Type	Year	Serial number	Notes
Maurice Farman Shorthorn	1916	CFS-20	• 30 percent original; purchased by R. G. Carey in 1919 for advertising use.

Maurice Farman Shorthorn at RAAF Museum

Museum Victoria

Nicholson Street
Carlton Gardens
Victoria 3015
AUSTRALIA

www.museumvictoria.com.au

Type	Year	Serial number	Notes
Duigan Biplane	1909		• First Australian-designed plane to achieve controlled, powered flight.

Museum of Applied Arts and Sciences (Powerhouse Museum)

500 Harris Street
Ultimo, Sydney
AUSTRALIA

www.powerhousemuseum.com

Type	Year	Serial number	Notes
Blériot XI	1914		• Flown by Maurice Guillaux. • First Melbourne-Sydney airmail flight. • Acquired by Powerhouse in 1941.

TVAL—The Vintage Aviator Ltd.

(Peter Jackson)

PO Box 14-458
Kilbirnie Wellington,
NEW ZEALAND

thevintageaviator.co.nz

Type	Year	Serial number	Notes
Bristol F.2B		D8084 S	• One of six fuselages found supporting a building. • Originally F4516.
RAF BE2C	1917	A1325	• Formerly owned by Mosquito, Norwegian, Guy Black. • On cover of *WWI Aero* magazine, No. 156, May 1997. • Purchased by 1914–1918 Heritage Trust. • Delivered to Norway in 1917.
Hanriot HD-1	1918	75	• Flown WWI: Jan Olieslager. • Restored by Marvin Hand. • Traded from the RAF Museum in 2013.
Sopwith Camel		N6254	• Formerly owned by W&W; Jarret; Tallman; Holbert Brothers; USMC Museum, Quantico, VA. • Formerly at Arkansas IMAX.
Avro 504K	1925	A202	• Owned by Aviation Historical Society, New Zealand. • Restored by the late Stuart Tantrum of Levin, NZ. • Exhibited at Omaka Airport, fully restored to flying status. • One of six purchased by New Zealand government in 1925.
Sopwith 1.5 Strutter			• From South America through New York auto dealer.

	• Restored by Century Aviation (Wenatchee, WA).
	• Traded from Kermit Weeks.
Henri Farman F.40	• Formerly owned by RAF Museum.

Omaka Aviation Heritage Centre

79 Aerodrome Road
Omaka, Blenheim 7272
NEW ZEALAND

www.omaka.org.nz

Type	Year	Serial number	Notes
Caproni Ca.22	1913		• Formerly: Caproni Museum.
De Havilland DH.4		AS 63786	• Built in the United States with v12 Liberty engine.
Curtiss MF Boat	1917	A5543	• From the Bonhams auction 2010, formerly owned by the Crawford Aviation Museum (Cleveland).
Thomas Morse Scout			

Museum of Transport and Technology (MOTAT)

190/200-208 Meola Road,
Western Springs, Auckland 1022
NEW ZEALAND

www.motat.org.nz

Type	Year	Serial number	Notes
Pearce Monoplane	1903		• Original parts. • Apparently flown before Wright brothers but without the ability to control the craft.

EUROPE

Heeresgeschichtliches Museum (Military History)

Arsenal Objekt 1
1030 Vienna
AUSTRIA

www.hgm.or.at

Type	Year	Serial number	Notes
French War Balloon	1796		• The French reconnaissance balloon called the L'Intrépide is the oldest existing flying device.
Albatros B.I	1913	20.01	• One of 5,200 aircraft used by the Austrian army and navy in World War I.

Original French War Balloon - Vienna

Techisches Museum

Mariahilfer Str. 212
1140 Vienna
AUSTRIA

www.technischesmuseum.at

Type	Year	Serial number	Notes
Aviatik (Berg) D.I	1918	"101.40"	
Etrich-II Taube	1910		• Donated by Igo Etrich in 1914.
Lilienthal Glider	1894		• Gifted in 1915 by Etrich Company
Pischof Monoplane	1910		• Donated in 1914 by the Austrian-Hungarian Autoplan Company.

The Royal Museum of the Armed Forces and Military History

Jubelpark 3
1000 Brussels
BELGIUM

www.klm-mra.be

Type	Year	Serial number	Notes
Aviatik C.1	1916	C227/16	• Restored at La Ferté Alais.
Battaille Triplane	1911		• Built by sculptor Cesar Battaille.
Blériot XI	1911		• Wings only, former parts from Jan Olieslager's plane.
Caudron G.3	1923	2351	
Farman MF.11 (Shorthorn)	1914		
Voisin LA.5b2	1911		• Fuselage only.
Halberstadt C.V	1918	3471/18	• Some sources say this is a Halberstadt D.IV.
Hanriot—Dupont HD-1	1918	HD-78	
LVG CVI	1918	5141/18	
Nieuport 23 C.1	1917	N5024	
RAF Re8	1917	8	• Bumblebee painted on fuselage
Schreck FBA Type H	1914	5.160	
Sopwith Camel	1917	B5747	
Sopwith 1.5 Strutter	1916	88	
SPAD S.XIII C.1	1918	SP-49	• Not listed everywhere.
Bristol F.2B Type 17			• One of the six supporting farmhouse (Weston-on-Green).
Zeppelin L-30			• Two of four nacelles.
Farman MF 20			• Fuselage only.

Letecke Muzeum (Prague Aviation Museum)

ul. Mladoboleslavská,
190 00 Praha 9-Kbely
CZECH REPUBLIC

www.vhu.cz/muzea/zakladni-informace-o-lm-kbely

Type	Year	Serial number	Notes
SPAD S.VII C1	1918	S11583	• Part of the T.S 16 Transport of June 6, 1919.
Letov S-2	1920		

National Technical Museum

Kostelní 1320/42
170 00 Praha-Holešovice
CZECH REPUBLIC

www.ntm.cz

Type	Year	Serial number	Notes
Anatra DS Anasal	1917	"11120"	
Hansa-Brandenburg D.1	1915	26.68	• Fuselage only.
Kaspar JK Monoplane	1911		
Knoller C.II	1915	119.15	
Morse LWF Model V Tractor	1918		
Praha Zenith Balloon	1904		• Both basket and balloon are original.
Zanonia Glider	1905		• Designed by Igo Etrich.

Danish Technical Museum

Fabriksvej 25
3000 Helsingør
DENMARK

www.tekniskmuseum.dk

Type	Year	Serial number	Notes
Donnet-Leveque II "Maagen 2"	1913		• Likely built at Franco-British Aviation in Vernon, France.
Ellehammer Helicopter	1912		
Ellehammer Monoplane	1909		
Farman Svendsen Glenten	1911		• Probably a copy of Henri Farman–Type Coupe Michelin

Danish Collection of Vintage Aircraft

6900 Skjern, Stauning
DENMARK

www.flymuseum.dk

Type	Year	Serial number	Notes
Berg Und Storm Monoplane	1911		• On loan from the National Defense History Museum, Copenhagen.
Avro 504N	1925	110	

The Imperial War Museum, Duxford—Fighter Collection

Duxford,
Cambridge CB22 4QR
ENGLAND

www.iwm.org.uk/visits/iwm-duxford

Type	Year	Serial number	Notes
Bristol F.2B (96)	1918	E2581	• Built by the British and Colonial Aeroplane Company at Filton.
DH.9	1918	D5649	• Restored by Guy Black.
RAF RE.8	1918	F3556	• Only complete RE.8 in existence.

Science Museum

Exhibition Road
London SW7 2DD
ENGLAND

www.sciencemuseum.org.uk

Type	Year	Serial number	Notes
Avro 504K	1918	D7560	
Cody V Biplane	1912	No. 304	
Fokker E.III	1916	210/16	• Only one of this type extant.
JAP Harding Monoplane	1910		• Blériot XI Type with 45-horsepower JAP V-8.
Antoinette Type VII	1910		
Lilienthal Standard XI	1895		
Roe Triplane 1	1909		
RAF SE5a	1918	687/F937	• Unacknowledged by museum.
Vickers Vimy	1919		• Alcock and Brown's plane.
Beta Airship Car Fuselage			

RAF Museum

Hendon: Grahame Park Way
London NW9 5LL
ENGLAND

Cosford: Shifnal
Shropshire TF11 8UP
ENGLAND

www.rafmuseum.org.uk

Type	Year	Serial number	Notes
Avro 504K	1918	E449/9205M	• Composite of two aircraft.
de Havilland DH.9A	1918	F1010	
Blériot XI	1910	164 9209M/BAPC	• Former Nash Collection (race car driver).
Blériot XXVII	1911	433	• Only one on earth.
Caudron G.3	1916	3066	
Clarke TWK Biplane Glider	1910	100	
Morane Saulnier BB	1916	A301	• In pieces and in storage in Stafford.
RAF SE5a	1918	F938	
Sopwith Pup	1916	N5182	• Doug Arnold traded a Spitfire to receive Pup. • One of two Pups and one Camel found in English barn by Desmond Saint Cyrien.
Fokker D.VII	1918	8417/18	• Formerly in Nash Collection.
Sopwith Triplane	1916	N5912	• Built by Oakley and Co. Ltd.
Sopwith Camel	1918	F6314	• F1 built by Boulton and Paul.
Bristol F.2B	1919	E2466	• One of six used in barn roof trusses.
RAF FE2b	1917	A6526	• Never completely built due to armistice.

			• Some consider this a reproduction built by John McKenzie in 2009.
Sopwith 5F.1 Dolphin	1918	C3988	• Original parts only. • Being restored by Michael Beetham Conservation Centre. • Only original Dolphin on earth.
Sopwith Snipe	1918	E6655	• Reconstructed with many original parts and engine. • 40 percent original; built by TVAL in New Zealand.
RAF R.E.8			• Original rudder, wing, and fuselage parts are in storage.
RAF BE2b		"687"	• Some consider this a replica. • Built from three original fuselage frames.

Imperial War Museum (London)

Lambeth Road
London SE1 6HZ
ENGLAND

www.iwm.org.uk

Type	Year	Serial number	Notes
SPAD S.VII	1917		• Formerly: Wings & Wheels(W&W). Incorrectly marked as SPAD S.XIII. • Some consider this a replica made in Germany.
Sopwith Camel	1918	6812	• Flown by Culley. • Shot down. • Zeppelin L53. • A William and Beardmore–built F1.
RAF BE2C	1916	2699	

Museum of Science and Industry (MOSI)

Liverpool Road
Manchester M3 4FP
ENGLAND

www.mosi.org.uk

Type	Year	Serial number	Notes
Avro 504K		G-ABAA	• On loan from the RAF Museum.

Shuttleworth Collection

SG18 9EP, Old Warden
ENGLAND

www.shuttleworth.org

Type	Year	Serial number	Notes
Avro 504K	1918	"E3273", (was "H5199")	• Won Devon race in 1937.
Blackburn Monoplane Type D	1912		• Formerly owned by Cyril Foggin, Francis Glew.
Bristol F.2B	1918	"D8096" "D"	• Served in Turkey. • Formerly owned by CPB Ogilvie.
Deperdussin	1910		• Formerly owned by A. E. Grimmer.
LVG C.VI	1918	"7198/18"	• Lent to RAF Museum (Cosford).
Blériot XI	1909	14	• Formerly at the Blériot school. • Oldest flying aircraft in the world.
Sopwith Pup	1916	"Happy" N6181	• Formerly Wylde. • Was converted to a Pup from a Dove in the thirties.
RAF SE5a	1917	"F904"	• Formerly owned by Major Savage.

Historic Aircraft Collection Limited (Guy Black)

New House, Northiam
Rye, East Sussex TN31 6JL
ENGLAND

www.historicaircraftcollection.ltd.uk

Type	Year	Serial number	Notes
DH.9		E-8894	• Formerly in palace's elephant stable, Junagarh Fort, Bikaner, India.

Fleet Air Arm Museum

RNAS Yeovilton Ilchester,
Somerset BA22 8HW
ENGLAND

www.fleetairarm.com

Type	Year	Serial number	Notes
Short 184	1915	8359	• Center section only (cockpit and engine). The rest was destroyed in London Blitz.
Sopwith Baby	1915	N2078	• This is a composite of two original aircraft; very little is original. • Apparently formerly of the Nash Collection.
Cody Kite			• This was likely an original "development kite."

Note: Museum displays the oldest aircraft carrier. It was towed behind destroyers in World War I as a takeoff platform.

The Museum of Army Flying

Middle Wallop
Stockbridge, Hampshire SO20 8DY
ENGLAND

www.armyflying.com

Type	Year	Serial number	Notes
Sopwith Pup	1916	N5195	• One of two Pups and one Camel found in English barn by Desmond Saint Cyrien. • Signed on stabilizer by Thomas Sopwith.

Private Ownership (Roy Palmer and Andy Saunders)

Weybridge
ENGLAND

Type	Year	Serial number	Notes
Sopwith Pup	1917	N6161	• Captured by Germans in 1917.

Private Ownership (Kelvyne Baker)

ENGLAND

Type	Year	Serial number	Notes
Sopwith Pup	1917	B1807	• An original that will be made flyable. • Found in a barn in Dorset, UK, in 1972. • To be exhibited at the Trust mansion and parklands of Tyntesfield.

Private Ownership (Family of Leslie Goldsmith)

ENGLAND

Type	Year	Serial number	Notes
Blériot XI			• Parts of three type-XI aircraft obtained by Leslie Goldsmith shortly after World War II.

Hallinportti Aviation Museum

Haukilahdentie 3
35600 Hall
Kuorevesi, Jämsä,
FINLAND

Type	Year	Serial number	Notes
Caudron G.3	1918	5A1	• Parts only.
Rumpler 6B.1	1918		• Only surviving floatplane.

The Aviation Museum of Central Finland (a.k.a. the Finnish Air Force Museum)

Tikkakoskentie 125
41160 Tikkakoski
FINLAND

www.airforcemuseum.fi

Type	Year	Serial number	Notes
Avro 504K	1917	E448	• In storage.
Martinsyde F.4 Buzzard	1918	MA-24	
Thulin D (Morane Parasol Type L)	1918	F.3	• Parts from wreckage. • There is also a full replica.
Bréguet 14 A2	1919	3C.30	

Musée Aéronautique de la Presqu'île Côte d'Amour

Aerodrome de La Baule
44500 La Baule Escoublac
Loire-Atlantique
FRANCE

www.mapica.org

Type	Year	Serial number	Notes
Blériot XI	1909	225	• One of only two originals still flying. • Presently back in the hands of Louis Blériot's grandson. • Blériot may also own a SPAD XIII.

Bleriot XI- Loire-Atlantique

Air Museum of Angers-Marcé

Angers-Loire Airport 49240 Marcé
FRANCE

www.musee-aviation-angers.fr

Type	Year	Serial number	Notes
Rene Gasnier III	1908		

Musée des Arts et Metiers (Museum of Arts and Crafts)

60, rue Réaumur
75003 Paris
FRANCE

www.arts-et-metiers.net

Type	Year	Serial number	Notes
Blériot XI	1909		• Original Channel crosser (unrestored).
Bréguet RU1	1911		
REP 1	1907		• Esnault Pelterie's plane.
Avion III	1897		• Clement Ader's plane.
Dufaux Helicopter	1905		• Pilotless.

Also noteworthy:
    Clement Ader's Avion II steam engine
    Gnome Delta Rotary engine (nine cylinders)

The Memorial Flight Association *(3 entities)*

Memorial Flight: 6 rue d'Artois, 91130 Ris Orangis
Salis: Aérodrome de Cerny-la Ferté-Alais
91590 Cerny
La-Ferté-Alais
FRANCE

www.memorial.flight.free.fr/indexuk.html

Jean Baptiste Salis

Type	Year	Serial number	Notes
Caudron G.3			• This is a replica but often erroneously called an original.

Les Casques de Cuir (Leather Helmet)

Type	Year	Serial number	Notes
Blériot XI	1909	877	• Crashed in English Channel during 1998 flight. • Many original parts.
Bristol F2B Fighter			• Called a reproduction.

Memorial Flight

Type	Year	Serial number	Notes
SPAD S.XIII	1918	"5"	• Donated to Memorial Flight by Jean Baptiste.
Morane A1 Type XXIX		1567	• No known history.
Sopwith 1 1/2 Strutter 1 B2	1917	2897	• Escadrille 66 paint (Indian bird). • Built by REP in 1917, 2897 is one of the 4,500 aircraft of this type built in France.

Sopwith 1B2 at Memorial Flight

Musée de l'Air et de l'Espace

Aéroport de Paris-Le Bourget,
93350 Le Bourget
FRANCE

www.museeairespace.fr

Type	Year	Serial number	Notes
Massia Biot (Glider)	1879		• Oldest heavier-than-air aircraft in a museum.
Blériot IX	1908		• Known as *Traversee de la Manche*
Blériot XI	1913	"PEGOUD"	
Blériot XI	1913		
Bréguet XIV A2	1917	"2016"	
Caudron G.3	1914	"ca. 329"	
Caudron G.4	1915	"ca. 1720"	
De Havilland DH.9	1917	"F1258"	
Deperdussin B	1911		
Deperdussin Mono	1913		
Donnet Leveque A	1912		
Fabre Hydravion	1910		• Acquired by the museum in 1920.
Farman F60 Goliath	1919		• Forward fuselage only.
Farman HF20	1913		
Farman MF 7	1911	"15" 446	• Fuselage only.
Fokker D.VII	1918	"6796/18"	• Acquired in 1920, this is the only example in the world.
Junkers J.9 (DI)	1918	D5929/18	

Levavasseur Antoinette VII	1909		• Fuselage and engine are original. • Wings built after World War II.
LVG C VI	1918	9041/18	
Morane Saulnier H	1913		
Nieuport 2N	1910		
Nieuport Delage XI	1915	N556 (formerly N976)	
Paumier Biplane	1912		
Pfalz D.XII	1918	2690/18	
Saconney Cerf Volant	1910		• Balloon basket with kite-like parachute.
Santos-Dumont Demoiselle	1908		
Sopwith 1.5 Strutter	1917	"556"	
SPAD S.VII	1916	S.254	• "Vieux Charles": Guynemer's plane. • Kept unrestored.
SPAD S.XIII C.1	1917	S5295	
Voisin Farman	1907 (1919)		• A replica, but interestingly, it was built in 1919 by museum staff.
Voisin 10 Ca2	1911		• Fully restored fuselage only, by Memorial Flight.
Voisin L.A.S	1915		
Vuia 1	1906		
Astra Wright Baby BB	1910		• French-copied version of Wrights' plane.
Chanute Glider			
REP (D)	1910		• Uncovered skeleton
REP (K)	1913		• Given to the museum by Robert Esnault-Pelterie (REP).
RAF BE2C		9969	• Stored.

Platform of Zeppelin LZ 113	1917		
Balloon Gondola	1918		
Morane-Saulnier AI XXIC C1	1921	2283	• Morane-Saulnier AI was built as an MoS XXIC C1, but it was used after the war by the aerobatics pilot Alfred Fronval and was modified for this use.

German Museum of Technology

Trebbiner Straße 9
10963 Berlin
GERMANY

www.sdtb.de

Type	Year	Serial number	Notes
Jeannin Stahl-Taube	1914		• Formerly in Krakow. • Came as part of a German-Polish restoration cooperation.
Junkers J4			• Fuselage only.
Pfalz D.VIII			• Only survivor, in pieces.
Halberstadt CL.IV	1918	"D71"	• Given to the museum by the USAF museum as payment for restoring three Paul Strahle original Halberstadts.

Verkehrsmuseum (Dresden Transport Museum)

Augustusstraße 1
01067 Dresden
GERMANY

www.verkehrsmuseum-dresden.de

Type	Year	Serial number	Notes
Grade Monoplane	1909		• Mostly made up of original parts. • The plane was received from Grade's widow.

Magdeburg Technical Museum

Lübeckerstraße 126,
39124 Magdeburg
GERMANY

www.technikmuseum-magdeburg.de

Type	Year	Serial number	Notes
Grade Monoplane	1909		• Restored in 2009 by Gerd Reinicke, using original parts.

Deutsches Museum (German Museum of Achievement in Science and Technology)

Museumsinsel 1,
80538 Munich
GERMANY

www.deutsches-museum.de

Type	Year	Serial number	Notes
Vollmoeller Monoplane	1910		• Fragments only.
Wolfmuller Glider	1907		
Wright Standard Type A	1909		• Only one in existence. • Original engine also displayed.
Grade Monoplane	1909		
Fokker D.VII	1918	4404/18	
Blériot XI	1909		• Formerly Dr. Paul Gens.
Etrich-Rumpler Taube	1910		• Helmut Hirth's Berlin-Munich flight.
Rumpler C.IV	1916		• One of only two that survive.
Gondola: "Parseval P.L.2"	1908		
Lilienthal (Normal-Segelapparat)	1894		• Its condition is bad and it's stored. • It is replaced in exhibition by a replica.

Auto Und Technick Museum

Eberhard-Layher-Straße 1,
74889 Sinsheim
GERMANY

www.sinsheim.technik-museum.de

Type	Year	Serial number	Notes
Hubner Eindekker	1911		• This was found in the early eighties and restored by museum members.

Private Ownership (Oliver Wulff)

St Augustin Hangelar
GERMANY

Type	Year	Serial number	Notes
Rumpler C.IV	1917	1463/17	• Formerly a part of Brussels collection. • Restored in Austria by Craft Lab from original parts.

Kozlekedesi (Transport) Museum

Budapest, Varosligeti korut 11, 1146
HUNGARY

www.mmkm.hu

Type	Year	Serial number	Notes
Lloyd	1914	40.01	• Fuselage received by museum in 1917 and restored in 1997.
Brandenburg B1	1914		

Museo del Risorgimento di Bergamo

Mercato del fieno
6/a Bergamo
ITALY

www.bergamoestoria.it

Type	Year	Serial number	Notes
Ansaldo A.1 Balilla	1918	16553	• Called "Saint George Project." • Restored by Turin chapter of GAVS.

Museo Vittoriale di Gardone

Via Vittoriale, 12,
25083 Gardone Riviera BS
ITALY

www.vittoriale.it

Type	Year	Serial number	Notes
Ansaldo SVA 5	1917	12736	• Restored in 1988.

Museo Baracca

Via Baracca 65
48022 Lugo
ITALY

www.museobaracca.it

Type	Year	Serial number	Notes
SPAD S.VII C.1	1917	S2489	• Used by 91st Squadron.

National Museum of Science and Technology "Leonardo da Vinci"

Via San Vittore
21, 20123 Milano
ITALY

www.museoscienza.org

Type	Year	Serial number	Notes
Nieuport 10		15179	• Macchi built.
Ricci R6 Triplane	1919		• A tiny aircraft with one of the shortest wingspans of the time.
Airship Gondola			

Museo del Genio Militare

Lungotevere delle Vittorie,
31, 00100 Rome
ITALY

www.esercito.difesa.it

Type	Year	Serial number	Notes
Blériot XI		4172	• It is not clear how much of this artifact is original, if any.

Museo Storico Italiano Della Guerra

Via Guglielmo Castelbarco
7, 38068 Rovereto TN
ITALY

www.museodellaguerra.it

Type	Year	Serial number	Notes
(Macchi) Nieuport 10	1916	13469	• In 1921, Emilio Strafelini donated it to the museum. • In 2005, it was restored by Marco Guerli.

Nieuport 10 - Rovereto

Parco e Museo del Volo Volandia

Area Ex Officine Aeronautiche Caproni 1910, via per Tornavento
15 Casenuove, 21019 Somma Lombardo VA
ITALY

www.volandia.it

Type	Year	Serial number	Notes
Gabardini Idrovolante			• On permanent loan from Caproni family.
Caproni Ca.1	1910		• Oldest plane in Italy, it was hidden at Caproni family estate during World War II. • It was moved to Volandia in 2007 and is on permanent loan from Caproni family.
Caproni Ca.18	1915		• On permanent loan from Caproni family.

Museo dell'Aeronautica Gianni Caproni

Via Lidorno
3, Trento
ITALY

www.museocaproni.it

Type	Year	Serial number	Notes
Ansaldo SVA 5	1918	11777	• Part of D'Annunzio's Vienna flights.
Ansaldo A.1 Balilla	1918	16553	• Owned by the city of Casale Monforatto, this plane was given to Captain Natali Palli at the end of the war.
Caproni Ca.6	1910		
Caproni Ca.9	1911		• Was on display in Washington, DC, at NASM for a time.
Caproni Ca.53 Triplane	1917		• Fuselage only. • In storage.
Caproni Bristol	1912		• Built in England. • One of the oldest British planes.
Fokker D.VIII	1920		• Only one known to exist. • No wings.
Huge Seatriplane (Ca.60)	1920		• Various parts from the destroyed plane.

Alenia Aermacchi Collection (formerly the Aeritalia Collection)

Turin
ITALY

www.aleniaaermacchi.it

Type	Year	Serial number	Notes
Ansaldo SVA 9		13148	• Plane was bought from Fyfield collection in 1989. • SVA stands for Savoia-Verduzio-Ansaldo.

Museum of the History of Italian Military Aviation

Strada Circumlacuale
00062 Vigna di Valle
Bracciano RM
ITALY

www.aeronautica.difesa.it/museovdv

Type	Year	Serial number	Notes
Ansaldo SVA 5	1918	11721	• Flown by Major Giordano Bruno Granzarolo.
Blériot XI (S.I.T)	1911		• Rare two-seat version.
Caproni Ca.36	1916	23174	• Flown by Lieutenant Casimiro Buttini.
Macchi-Hanriot HD-1	1916	HD.19309	• Flown by Flavio Torello Baracchini.
Lohner L.I	1917	"L127"	• World's only example.
SPAD S.VII	1917	S1420	• Flown by Ernesto Cabruno.
SPAD S.VII	1916	S.1353 "S.153"	• Flown by Fulco Ruffo. • Oldest SPAD in the world.
Balloon	1804		• Colonel Garnerin's balloon.

Rijksmuseum

Postbus 74888
1070 DN Amsterdam
NETHERLANDS

www.rijksmuseum.nl

Type	Year	Serial number	Notes
F.K. 23 Bantam	1917		• Formerly owned by Captain Ogilvie, Aviodrome, and Shuttleworth. • Last existing aircraft of Frederick Koolhoven.

Louwman Collection

Leidsestraatweg 57
2594 BB The Hague
NETHERLANDS

www.louwmanmuseum.nl

Type	Year	Serial number	Notes
Blériot XI	1909		
Farman HF 20	1913		• Called a "reconstruction" by the museum.
R34 Gondola (British)	1918		

Aviodrome

Pelikaanweg 50,
8218 PG Lelystad
NETHERLANDS

www.aviodrome.nl

Type	Year	Serial number	Notes
Fokker Spin	1912		• Plane was put together from parts in the twenties.

Museum of Military Aviation

Kampweg 120,
3769 DJ, Soesterberg
NETHERLANDS

info@militaireluchtvaartmuseum.nl

Type	Year	Serial number	Notes
Fokker D.VII	1918	"266" 2528/18	• Formerly Wings & Wheels, Fokker Co. • Aviodrome had it on loan for a time. • Part of Early Birds Foundation. • Formerly Tallmantz. • Restored by Dick Funcke.

Norwegian Aviation Museum

Olav V gate,
8004 Bodø
NORWAY

www.luftfartsmuseum.no

Type	Year	Serial number	Notes
Avro 504K	1917	"103"	<ul><li>Known as a "Dyak."</li><li>Engine is a Sunbeam Dyak.</li><li>Assembled at the Kjeller aircraft factory and delivered to the Sønnenfjeldske Flying Unit in July 1921.</li></ul>
Hanover CL.V "Hawk"	1920–1924		<ul><li>Fuselage only.</li><li>License built by Kjeller Flyfabrikk.</li></ul>

Forsvarets Flysamling—Norwegian Armed Forces Aircraft Collection

Oslo-Gardermoen Airport
Museumsvegen 180
2060 Gardermoen
NORWAY

www.flysam.no

Type	Year	Serial number	Notes
RAF Be2e	1916	A1380	• Scottish built by subcontractor William Denny in 1916 and arrived at Kjeller, Norway, on September 5, 1917.
Rumpler Taube	1912	"START"	• Built in Germany and made its first flight in Norway, flown by Lieutenant Hans Fleischer Dons. • On loan from Technical Museum, Oslo.
Farman F-46E (Ecole)	1920		

Norwegian Technical Museum

Kjelsåsveien 143
0491 Oslo
NORWAY

www.tekniskmuseum.no

Type	Year	Serial number	Notes
Maurice Farman MF7 (Longhorn)	1913		
Haereas Flyvemaskinfabrik			• Fuselage only. • Hannover CL.V licensed and built.
Blériot XI	1914	794	• Flown by Lt. Trygve Gran "Nordsjoen."
Deperdussin A	1913		

Museum of Aviation and Space

Aleja Jana Pawła II 39
31-864 Kraków
POLAND

www.muzeumlotnictwa.pl

Type	Year	Serial number	Notes
Albatros C.I	1915	197/15	
Albatros H.1	1918	10114	
AEG-Wagner Eule	1914		
Aviatik C.III	1917	C12250/17	• Last on earth.
DFW C.V	1917	17077/17	• Last on earth.
Geest Mowe IV Monoplane	1913		• Last on earth.
Grigorovich M-15	1917	R II C 262	• Last on earth.
Levavasseur Antoinette	1909		
LFG Roland D.VI	1918	D2225/18	• No wings • Only surviving example.
LVG B.II	1917	350/17	• Last on earth.
Sopwith Camel	1917	B7280	• Shot down eleven enemy planes.
Staaken R VI	1917		• Just one nacelle in poor condition.
Albatros B. IIa (L.30)	1919	10019	
Halberstadt CL.II	1917	15459/17	

The Technical Museum

plac Defilad 1, Warsaw
POLAND

www.mtip.pl

Type	Year	Serial number	Notes
Lilienthal Monoplane Glider	1894		• Restored in 2012 at the Museum of Aviation and Astronautics in Krakow, Poland. • 90 percent of its components are original.

Museo de Marinha

Praça do Império,
1400-206 Lisbon
PORTUGAL

museu.marinha.pt

Type	Year	Serial number	Notes
Shreck FBA Type B	1914	"2"	
Fairey D	1922	F402	• Used for Portugal-to-Rio flight.

The Central Museum of the Air Forces

Muzeynaya ulitsa,
1, Monino, 141170
RUSSIA

www.moninoaviation.com

Type	Year	Serial number	Notes
Sopwith Triplane	1917	N5486	• Supplied to Russia for evaluation. • Fitted with skis and used extensively. • Captured by Bolshevists. • Rebuilt many times in early years.

Shukowski Museum

Moscow
RUSSIA

Type	Year	Serial number	Notes
Lilienthal Glider			• There is very little written about this aircraft.

Museum of Scotland

East Fortune Airfield,
East Lothian EH39 5LF
SCOTLAND

www.nms.ac.uk/national-museum-of-flight

Type	Year	Serial number	Notes
Airship R34	1918		• Many parts.
Percy Pilcher's "Hawk Glider"	1896		• In storage.
Sopwith Cuckoo Mk.1	1918		• Wings only.
RAF SE5a	1918	9084 & 5636	• Wings only.

Museo del Aire

Autovía de Extremadura
Km 10,500, 28024 Madrid
SPAIN

www.ejercitodelaire.mde.es

Type	Year	Serial number	Notes
Blériot XI	1911		• The Vilanova Acedo is the oldest aircraft in Spain.

Landskrona Museum

Slottsgatan
261 31 Landskrona
SWEDEN

www.landskrona.se/museum.aspx

Type	Year	Serial number	Notes
Thulin Type NA	1918		
Thulin B			• Wings only.

Thulin NA at Landskrona Museum

Malmen Air Force Museum

Carl Cederstroms gata,
Malmslatt, Linköping
SWEDEN

www.flygvapenmuseum.se/en

Type	Year	Serial number	Notes
Macchi M7	1918	"945"	• Last on earth.
Phonix 122 DIII	1920		
Thulin G	1917		
Albatros SK.1 (like BII)	1925		
Bréguet BI	1912		• Last on earth.
Donnet-Leveque ("Flying Fish")	1913		• Formerly at Sweden's Technical Museum in Stockholm.

Private Ownership (Mikael Carlson)

Kvarnhem, Sebbarp
SE-240 33 Löberöd
SWEDEN

www.aerodrome.se

Type	Year	Serial number	Notes
Thulin A	1918		• Plane was found in barn in late eighties.
Thulin A	1918		• Just like a Blériot XI. • Both are from the same batch of ten built by Aktiebolaget Enoch Thulin's Aeroplanfabrik (AETA) in 1918.

Carlson's Thulin A's

Tekniska Museet

Malmöhusvägen 7A,
211 18 Malmö
SWEDEN

www.tekniskamuseet.se

Type	Year	Serial number	Notes
Thulin Type B	1916		• On loan from Stockholm museum.
Thulin Type A	1917		• Fuselage only.

Museum of Science and Industry

Museivägen 7,
Gärdet, Stockholm
SWEDEN

www.tekniskamuseet.se

Type	Year	Serial number	Notes
Blériot XI	1918		• Purchased by Thulin and christened *Nordstiernan*.
(Nyrop No. 3) Blériot XI copy	1911		• Built by Hjalmar Nyrop, this is the oldest plane in Sweden.
Thulin Type N	1917		• With pontoons.
Berger Bo	1911		• Unsuccessful steam plane.

Svedino's Auto-Aviation Museum

SE-311 69 Ugglarp
SWEDEN

www.svedinos.se/en

Type	Year	Serial number	Notes
Thulin A	1918	16	• 40 to 50 percent original.

Aviation Museum Dubendorf (Flieger Flab)

Überlandstrasse 255
CH-8600 Dübendorf
SWITZERLAND

www.airforcecenter.ch

Type	Year	Serial number	Notes
Hanriot HD.1		"653"	• Macchi built.
Nieuport 28. C1		"607"	• Original serial number 6212.
Fokker D.VII		"640"	• Replica with some original parts.

Swiss Museum of Transport

Lidostrasse 5,
6006 Lucerne
SWITZERLAND

www.verkehrshaus.ch

Type	Year	Serial number	Notes
Blériot XI-B	1913		• Flown by Oscar Bider.
Dufaux IV	1910		
Nieuport 28C	1918	688	
Rech Monoplane	1912		• In storage.

National Waterfront Museum

Former holdings of RAF Saint Athan, this is apparently a Hendon overflow, but it is no longer used.

Oystermouth Road,
Swansea SA1 3rd
WALES

www.museumwales.ac.uk/en/swansea

Type	Year	Serial number	Notes
Watkins CHW Monoplane	1908	⟨	• On loan from the National Museum, Wales.

NORTH AMERICA

Base Borden Military Museum

CFB Borden, Barrie, Ontario
CANADA

www.cg.cfpsa.ca

Type	Year	Serial number	Notes
Avro 504K	1918	G-CYCK	• The oldest flyable aircraft in Canada. • It is Major Appleby's aircraft, now on loan from Rockcliffe.

Private Ownership (John F. Johnson)

Edmonton
CANADA

Type	Year	Serial number	Notes
Curtiss JN-4D		3973	

The Tiger Boys

304 Stone Road West
Guelph, Ontario N1G 4W4
CANADA

www.tigerboys.com

Type	Year	Serial number	Notes
Curtiss JN-4C (Canuck)			

Brome County Historical Society

Centennial Building
130 Lakeside, Knowlton Quebec
CANADA

www.bromemuseum.com

Type	Year	Serial number	Notes
Fokker D.VII	1918	6810/18	• Considered the most complete example of the D.VII in the world with original fabric featuring Lozenge pattern.

Fokker D.VII in Brome County

Canadian War Museum

1 Vimy Place
Ottawa, ON K1A
CANADA

www.warmuseum.ca

Type	Year	Serial number	Notes
Sopwith Snipe	1918	E8102	• Fuselage of Barker's plane, flown in October 1918.

Canada's Aviation and Space Museum

11 Aviation Parkway
Rockcliffe, Ottawa
CANADA

www.casmuseum.techno-science.ca

Type	Year	Serial number	Notes
AEG GIV	1918	6574/18 IV	
Avro 504K	1917	D8971	• Formerly Rhinebeck.
Curtiss JN-4C	1918	C227	• Formerly George Reese, Ed Faulkner.
Curtiss HS-2L	1918	A1876	• "Laurentide Air Service" • Built from underwater remains of La Vigilance. • Combination of two HS-2Ls.
Maurice Farman S.11 Shorthorn	1915		• Formerly Frank Tallman, W&W.
Fokker D.VII	1918	10347/18	• Formerly Howard Hughes. • Used in *Hells Angels*. • Formerly owned by Jim Nissen.
Junkers J.1	1918	586/18	• Only complete example in existence.
McDowall Monoplane	1915		• Formerly owned by Ed Platt and then Keith Hopkinson.
Nieuport 12	1915		• Gift to Canada from France.
RAF B.E.2c	1915	5878	• Originally misidentified as plane that shot down Zep L32 by Lt. F. Sowery.
Sopwith F.1 Ship Camel	1917	N8156	• Was displayed at Canadian War Museum.
Sopwith Snipe	1918	E6938	• Formerly owned by Reginald Denny, Jack Canary.
SPAD S.VII C1	1917	B9913	• Formerly at Dayton, W&W, Balboni, Jarret, Tallman, Bob Rust, JB Petty.

			• Will be transferred to another museum at some point in the future.
Blériot XI	1911		• Built for John W. Hamilton. • Believed first Cali-built airplane to fly.
Curtiss Seagull	1920		• Explored Amazon River in 1924.
Borel-Morane	1912		• Bought from Earl Daugherty estate in September 2002.
Bristol F.2b		D7889	• Acquired through trade with Guy Black.

Reynolds-Alberta Museum

6426 40 Avenue
Wetaskiwin, Alberta T9A 0N3
CANADA

www.history.alberta.ca/reynolds

Type	Year	Serial number	Notes
Curtiss JN-4C (Canuck)	1918	c1347	
Reynolds Sport	1919		• Ted Reynolds built it with a Fokker Eindecker in mind.
Curtiss Pusher	1911		• Partially original (wheels, engine, and some other things).

Mexico City Airport

Av Capitan Carlos León S/N
Venustiano Carranza, Peñón de los Baños,
15620 Ciudad de México, D.F.
MEXICO

www.aicm.com.mx

Type	Year	Serial number	Notes
Lincoln Standard J-1 Speedster	1922		• Flown by Compañía Mexicana de Aviación.

US Army Aviation Museum

Army Aviation Museum Foundation, Inc.
6000 Novosel St.
Fort Rucker, AL 36362

www.armyaviationmuseum.org

Type	Year	Serial number	Notes
Sopwith Camel		"4"	• Restored by A.J.D. Engineering, Ltd. (Anthony Dithridge) in 1985, using all original parts, but it is not an attributable airframe. • Built by workers from the original Sopwith Aviation Company, Ltd. • Staff calls this aircraft "Frankenstein."
Curtiss JN-4	1917	278 "525"	• Formerly Harrah's Reno Auto Collection.
Nieuport 28C	1917	6531	• Guy Black restored. • Formerly owned by W&W. • Used in the film *Dawn Patrol*.
WWI Balloon Basket			

Alaska Aviation Heritage Museum

4721 Aircraft Drive (Lake Hood)
Anchorage, AK 99502-1052

Type	Year	Serial number	Notes
Douglas World Cruiser ("Seattle")	1924		• Recovered in the sixties by Bob Reeve.

Douglass World Cruiser Seattle

Fairbanks International Airport Terminal

6450 Airport Way,
Fairbanks, AK 99709

Type	Year	Serial number	Notes
Curtiss JN-4D		4735	• "Fairbanks" • Formerly owned by Carl Ben Eielson. • Apparently viewable since 1981, now newly restored.

Sky Harbor International Airport

(Owned by the city of Phoenix, Arizona)

3400 East Sky Harbor Boulevard
Phoenix, AZ 85034

Type	Year	Serial number	Notes
SPAD S.XIII			• 90 percent original. • Formerly owned by Tillamook AFB. • Restored by GossHawk Unlimited (Arizona).

Planes of Fame

7000 Merrill Avenue No.17
Chino, CA 91710

www.planesoffame.org

Type	Year	Serial number	Notes
Hanriot HD-1	1918	5624	• Nungesser's plane, which was used in the film *Dawn Patrol*.

Yanks Air Museum

7000 Merrill Ave #35-A270
Chino, CA 91710

www.yanksair.com

Type	Year	Serial number	Notes
Thomas Pigeon Flying Boat	1920		• Formerly owned by Fyfield, Cole Palen. • Was in Pigeon Brothers' factory rafters.
Curtiss JN-4D	1917	N1563 D51	
Thomas-Morse S-4C	1918	38734	• Purchased from sale in 2008. • Yet another aircraft used in film *Dawn Patrol*.
Unknown early original			• Single-seater.
Standard J-1			• Considered partially original. • Original Hall Scott A-7-A.

Private Ownership (David Baumbach)

Ione
CALIFORNIA

Type	Year	Serial number	Notes
Curtiss JN-4D	1917	"996"	• Formerly owned by Yanks (Chino). • Navy type.

California Science Center

700 Exposition Park Drive
Los Angeles, CA 90037

www.californiasciencecenter.org

Type	Year	Serial number	Notes
Curtiss JN-4			• Formerly owned by Yanks, and apparently will be at museum around 2018.

Aeroplane Collection (Privately Owned by Javier Arango)

Paso Robles, CA

Type	Year	Serial number	Notes
Blériot XI	1911		• Formerly owned by Vandersaal Brothers in Colorado. • Formerly at Raceway Equipment in Alabama, then G. Martin of Villadossoia, Italy.
Sopwith Camel	1917	B6291	• Was on loan from AJD Engineering. • Shuttleworth sale, sold to Al Lechter in California. • Formerly owned by Desmond Saint Cyrien. • Formerly at Army Museum of Flying.

Hiller Aviation Museum

601 Skyway Rd.
San Carlos, CA 94070

www.hiller.org

Type	Year	Serial number	Notes
Black Diamond	1910		• On loan from NASM. • Maupin/Lanteri plane.
Little Looper	1914		• Lincoln Beachey.

San Diego Air and Space Museum

2001 Pan American Plaza
San Diego, CA 92101
Balboa Park, San Diego, CA
(Also in the annex at Gillespie Field)
San Diego, CA

www.sandiegoairandspace.org

Type	Year	Serial number	Notes
Curtiss JN-4D	1918	"38262"	• Completely rebuilt from crashed plane. • Formerly in Mantz, John Larsen collection. • Used by Lindbergh in movie *Spirit of Saint Louis*.
Deperdussin Militaire	1911	no markings	• Formerly owned by Salis, W&W.
Nieuport 28C.1	1918	"6" 6169	• Formerly Tallmantz (parts for one and a half planes). • Hunt and R. Folsom built repro from original parts.
SPAD S.VII	1917	B9916	• Formerly owned by NASM, W&W, Swede/Ralston.
Standard J-1 (Lincoln type)	1918	2826 (5083)	• Painted "Sky rides, Spectacular & Safe." • Formerly at Rhinebeck.
Montgomery Evergreen Glider	1912		• On loan from NASM.
Blériot XI	1910		• Rebuilt from original parts by John Russell.
Balloon Basket	1918		

Museum of Flying

3100 Airport Avenue
Santa Monica, CA 90405

Type	Year	Serial number	Notes
Douglas World Cruiser	1923	*New Orleans*	• Once on loan to USAF Museum, Dayton from the Los Angeles County Natural History Museum.

Private Ownership (Walt Bowe)

Sonoma, CA

Type	Year	Serial number	Notes
Standard J-1	1917	2969	• Formerly at Golden Age Air Museum.

Private Ownership (Frank Schelling)

Sonoma Valley Airport
Schellville, CA

Type	Year	Serial number	Notes
Curtiss JN-4H	1918	3223	

Nut Tree Center for Patriotism (Doolittle Center)

300 County Airport Road
Vacaville, CA 95688

www.doolittlecenter.org

Type	Year	Serial number	Notes
Gonzales Biplane	1912		• Formerly on loan to Hiller.

Gonzales Biplane at the Nut Tree Center

Denver International Airport (Antique Airplane Association of Colorado)

Denver, CO

Type	Year	Serial number	Notes
Curtiss JN-4D	1918	"65" SC1918	• Displayed in concourse B.

New England Air Museum

36 Perimeter Rd.
Bradley International Airport
Windsor Locks, CT 06096

www.neam.org

Type	Year	Serial number	Notes
Blériot XI	1911	"Ernest No. 1"	• Gift of United Technologies. • Ernest Hall's aircraft.
Brooks Balloon Basket	circa 1870		
Nixon Homebuilt	1919		
Chalais Meudon	1918	CM-5	• Found at Goodyear Hangar (Nacelle).
Curtiss JN-4D			
Curtiss JN-4C			
Bunce Built Curtiss Pusher	1912		• Built by Connecticut local in about 1912, it is the oldest Connecticut airplane.

National Naval Aviation Museum

1750 Radford Boulevard
Pensacola, FL 32506

www.navalaviationmuseum.org

Type	Year	Serial number	Notes
Curtiss JN-4D	1917	"995"	• Uncovered (partially).
Curtiss (MF) Boat	1918	A5483	
Curtiss 12 (NC-4)	1918	"4" A-2294	• On loan from NASM.
Thomas Morse S-4C Scout	1918	"A-5858"	• Received from California's Rockwell Field.
Hanriot HD-1	1919	"A5625"	• Considered a replica built from several original parts. • On loan from USMC Air-Ground Museum.
Nieuport 28	1919	"21" 5796	• On loan from Howard Wells, Sepulveda, CA.
Sopwith Camel	1917	A5658	• "TEXAS" • On loan from Howard Wells, Sepulveda, CA.
Balloon Gondola	1917		• Used in France in World War I.

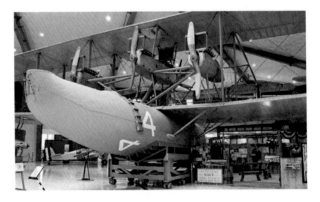

Curtiss NC-4 in Pensacola

Fantasy of Flight (Kermit Weeks Collection)

1400 Broadway Blvd SE
Polk City, FL 33868

www.fantasyofflight.com

Type	Year	Serial number	Notes
Avro 504J/K	1916	B3182	• Oldest surviving 504. • Acquired at a Boise auction and converted from a "J" type.
Orenco F	1917	N2145	• Formerly owned by Tallmantz. • Only surviving example.
Standard J-1	1917	N2825D (1582)	• Formerly owned by Tallmantz.
Thomas Morse Scout		633 (Sc-44610)	• Formerly owned by Jarrett, Crawford Museum.
Morane A1	1918		• Formerly Tallmantz collection.
De Havilland DH.4		358	• Apparently, three are owned.
Curtiss JN-4D		N2404	• Restored by Century Aviation.
Standard E-1		49128	• Formerly at USAF Museum.
Morane (Brock)	1916		• Formerly at Museum of Science and Industry, Chicago.

Candler Field Museum

Candler Field
Williamson, GA 30292

www.peachstateaero.com/museum

Type	Year	Serial number	Notes
Curtiss JN-4	1918	"Candler Field"	• Being restored by Brian Karli. • Website: curtissjennyrestoration.blogspot.com • Formerly at Paul Dougherty's Golden Age, Bethel, PA.

Museum of Science and Industry

5700 S. Lake Shore Drive
Chicago, IL 60637

www.msichicago.org

Type	Year	Serial number	Notes
Curtiss JN-4D	1917	5368	• Restored by Century Aviation.

National Motorcycle Museum

102 Chamber Drive
Anamosa, IA 52205

www.nationalmcmuseum.org

Type	Year	Serial number	Notes
Steco (Stephens Co.)	1911		• Found completely intact in crates by Dennis Eggert, who donated it to NMM.

State Historical Museum of Iowa

600 East Locust St.
Des Moines, IA 50319

www.iowahistory.org

Type	Year	Serial number	Notes
Blériot XI	1909		• Evert "Hud" Weeks restored it in the late fifties and early sixties.
Curtiss Klein Pusher Biplane	1911		• Built from a kit by brothers Arthur and Ben Klein in Treynor, Iowa.
Benoist Tractor Biplane	1917		• Built and flown by Lt. Oscar Solbrig, known as the Davenport Bird Man, and restored by Louis Anderson.

Frontier Army Museum

100 Reynolds Avenue
Fort Leavenworth, KS 66027

www.ffam.us

Type	Year	Serial number	Notes
Curtiss JN-4D		95371	

Kansas State Historical Society

6425 SW 6th Avenue
Topeka, KS 66615-1099

www.kshs.org

Type	Year	Serial number	Notes
Longren Biplane	1914		• One of twenty-one different aircraft built before Longren Co. closed in 1923.

Owls Head Transportation Museum

117 Museum Street
Owls Head, ME 04854

www.owlshead.org

Type	Year	Serial number	Notes
Curtiss JN-4S	1917	34094	
Standard J-1	1918	581	• Jones formerly owned by N. S. Sorensen. • Formerly owned by Chet Peek, who found it in a Nebraska haystack in 1954.
Clark Ornithopter	1900		• Unsuccessful craft built by clockmaker James Clark.

College Park Aviation Museum

1985 Corporal Frank Scott Dr.
College Park, MD 20740

www.collegeparkaviationmuseum.com

Type	Year	Serial number	Notes
Curtiss JN-4D	1916		• Restored by Ken Hyde and on loan to the College Park Aviation Museum from the US Army Center for Military History. • Parts found in San Antonio, TX (60 percent).
Nieuport 23 (Berliner Helicopter)			• Original N23 fuselage used in helicopter experiments. • On loan from NASM.

Bob Collings Foundation

137 Barton Road
PO Box 248
Stow, MA 01775

www.collingsfoundation.org

Type	Year	Serial number	Notes
Blériot XI	1909		
Curtiss Pusher	1909		• Restored by Century Aviation.

The Henry Ford

20900 Oakwood Boulevard
Dearborn, MI 48124-5029

www.thehenryford.org

Type	Year	Serial number	Notes
Curtiss JN-4C	1917	8428	• Canuck, painted like a fish. • A gift from Ray Dahlinger.
Laird Biplane	1915		• Piloted by Katherine Stinson.
Blériot XI	1910		
Dayton-Wright RB-1 (racer)	1920		

Fagen Fighters WWII Museum

2450 540th Street
Granite Falls, MN 56241

www.fagenfighterswwiimuseum.org

Type	Year	Serial number	Notes
Curtiss JN-4D	1917	450 (2975)	• Sold by K. Hyde. • Formerly at Virginia Air Museum.

Historic Aircraft Restoration Museum (Al Stix)

3127 Creve Coeur Mill Road
Saint Louis, MO 63146

www.historicaircraftrestorationmuseum.org

Type	Year	Serial number	Notes
Curtiss JN-4C	1916	c496	• Made by Canadian Aeroplane Co. • Restored by Don Hegebuth and Bob Daniels.
Standard J-1	1917	N62505	• Considered the only flying example. • Formerly owned Ray Folsom.
DH.4M2	1920		• Built by Fokker Atlantic in America after 1919 and restored over thirty years, using parts from many Fokker DH.4s.

Stonehenge Air Museum (Jim Smith Collection)

Crystal Lake, MT

www.stonehengeairmuseum@gmail.com

Type	Year	Serial number	Notes
Curtiss JN-4D	1917		• Formerly Mantz owned. • Comes from Benjamin Bower of Knoxville, Tennessee, who bought two dozen Jennies from John Wyche of Macon, Georgia. Wyche had earlier purchased all 160 surplus Jennies from the army at Southern Field, Americus, Georgia.

Dawson County Historical Museum

805 Taft Street
Lexington, NE 68850

www.dchsmuseum.com

Type	Year	Serial number	Notes
McCabe Baby Biplane	1919	841	• It apparently flew. • Planned as a kit airplane for use on submarines.

McCabe Baby Biplane in Dawson County

Harold Warp Pioneer Village

138 E US Highway 6
Minden, NE 68959

www.pioneervillage.org

Type	Year	Serial number	Notes
WWI observation balloon			• Basket only.
Curtiss Pusher D	1910		• Flown by Hamilton on a New York–Philadelphia run.
Curtiss JN-4D	1917	1350	• Formerly owned by Virgil King, Pennsylvania.
Hartman Monoplane	1910	N286Y	• Greatly altered aluminum tubing, etc. • First to fly in Iowa.
1903 Kitty Hawk Flyer (early replica)			• Built from memory by Orville Wright in 1914.
Lincoln Standard J-1	1918		• Not in displayable condition, although the Standard's Renault engine is on display. • Acquired in Nebraska in 1954 from James Marshall.

Albuquerque International Airport (Sunport)

2200 Sunport SE
Albuquerque, NM

Type	Year	Serial number	Notes
Ingram Foster (Curtiss Biplane)	1911		

Cradle of Aviation Museum

Charles Lindbergh Boulevard
Garden City, NY 11530

www.cradleofaviation.org

Type	Year	Serial number	Notes
Breese Penguin	1917	33622	• Formerly owned by W&W • Only example extant.
Curtiss JN-4	1918		• Flown by Charles Lindbergh.
Curtiss JN-4			• Fuselage, tail surfaces, and wing, left uncovered. • Partially original.
ACE (Aircraft Engineering Corp.)	1918		• On loan: Friends for LI Heritage. • Formerly at Owls Head.
Thomas Morse S4C (2)	1918		• On loan from Paul Kotze.
Blériot XI	1909	153	• Formerly in Rhinebeck. • Imported by Rodman Wanamaker.
Timmons Kite	1906		• Built and flown in South Ozone Park, Queens.

Glenn H. Curtiss Museum

8419 State Route 54
Hammondsport, NY 14840

www.glennhcurtissmuseum.org

Type	Year	Serial number	Notes
Curtiss JN-4D	1918		
Unknown early aircraft			• Found in barn, the museum staff feels it isn't a Jenny or a homebuilt. • In storage.
Curtiss Seagull Flying Boat	1919	257	• On loan from Henry Ford Museum.
Standard J-1	1916	823H	• On loan from Henry Ford Museum.

Engines in Glenn H. Curtiss Museum's collection

- 1912 60-horsepower Curtiss Model S—straight six
- 1914 200-horsepower Curtiss V2C10-V8
- 1916 90-horsepower Lawrence two-cylinder, opposed
- 1917 100-horsepower Gnome nine-cylinder rotary
- 1917 110-horsepower LeRhone nine-cylinder rotary
- 1918 90-horsepower Curtiss OX-5-V8
- 1918 400-horsepower Liberty—V12
- 1918 150-horsepower Kirkham—straight six
- 1910 20-horsepower Aero-Sled—two-cylinder, opposed

Ithaca Aviation Heritage Foundation (IAHF)

Ithaca, NY

www.tommycomehome.org

Type	Year	Serial number	Notes
Thomas-Morse S-4B	1918	34544	• Plane donated to IAHF in 2010 by Dr. William N. Thibault of San Diego. • Built in the city of Ithaca, it was thought to have been a more common S-4C. • It was a part of the San Diego Air and Space Museum for years.

Niagara Aerospace Museum

9900 Porter Road
Niagara Falls International Airport
Niagara Falls, NY 14304

www.wnyaerospace.org

Type	Year	Serial number	Notes
Curtiss JN-4	1917	3407	• Found and purchased in Ohio.

Old Rhinebeck Aerodrome

9 Norton Road
Red Hook, NY 12571

www.oldrhinebeck.org

Type	Year	Serial number	Notes
Blériot XI	1909	"7" #56	• Formerly owned by Bill Champlin, Professor Coburn. • Oldest flying aircraft in United States. • Some have speculated that this was Harriet Quimby's plane.
Blériot XI	1911	N99923	• Formerly owned by James McGrath.
Albree Pigeon Fraser	1917		
Burgess Collier Model M Flying Boat	1911		• Wings only. • Only one in the world.
Curtiss JN-4H	1917	38262	• "United States Navy"
Morane Saulnier A.I	1917	MS1591	• Formerly owned by W&W.
Nieuport 10 (also a.k.a. 83)	1912		• Formerly owned by Nungesser.
Thomas Pusher E	1912		• Formerly owned by Owen Billman, Earl Frits.
Thomas Morse S-4B	1917	4328	• Apparently, only surviving example. • Formerly owned by Roland Jack, Frank Sharpless, Woodward.
Voisin	1908		• Displayed on the *Intrepid* at one point.
Aeromarine 39B	1918		• Parts only. • Burned while being moved to Florida. • Last known original.

Empire State Aerosciences Museum

250 Rudy Chase Drive
Scotia, NY 12302

www.esam.org

Type	Year	Serial number	Notes
Von Pomer Biplane	1910		• Partial original with mocked-up engine.
Chanute Style Glider	1896		• Plane flown by Owen Billman. • Found in carriage house in Amsterdam, NY, in 1950.

Fargo Air Museum

1609 Nineteenth Avenue North
Fargo, ND 58102

www.fargoairmuseum.org

Type	Year	Serial number	Notes
Standard J-1	1917	N9477 (2434)	• Charles Klessig rebuilt and restored it in 1971. • Semioriginal. • On loan from Cass County Historical Society.

Bonanzaville Museum

1351 Main Avenue W
West Fargo, ND 58078

www.bonanzaville.org

Type	Year	Serial number	Notes
Curtiss Pusher D3	1911		• Restored in 1981 by Charles Klessig.

Crawford Auto-Aviation Museum (Western Reserve)

10825 East Boulevard
Cleveland, OH 44106

www.info@wrhs.org

Type	Year	Serial number	Notes
Curtiss Model E	1910		• "Bumble Bee" • Only Curtiss hydro on earth. • Formerly owned by Al Engel.

Ohio History Connection

800 E. Seventeenth Avenue
Columbus, OH 43211

www.ohiohistory.org

Type	Year	Serial number	Notes
Wilbur-Curtiss Pusher	1911		• Lent to Liberty Aviation Museum, Ohio.

Carillon Historical Park

1000 Carillon Boulevard
Dayton, OH 45409

www.daytonhistory.org

Type	Year	Serial number	Notes
Wright Flyer III	1905		• Used for testing at Huffman Prairie. • Rebuilt and restored by Orville Wright.

National Museum of the USAF

1100 Spaatz Street
Dayton, OH 45431

www.nationalmuseum.af.mil

Type	Year	Serial number	Notes
Blériot XI	1909		• Ernest Hall built this plane.
Curtiss JN-4D	1917	2805	• Formerly owned by Robert Pfeil and acquired in 1956.
Halberstadt CL.IV	1918	8103/18	
SPAD S.VII	1916	AS94099	• Formerly at Science and Industry Museum in Chicago.
Standard J-1	1918	22692	• Restored by Dayton Museum in 1981.
Thomas Morse S4C	1917	SC38944	• Formerly owned by R. W. Duff.
RAF SE5e (Eberhart)		22–325	• Formerly owned by Tallmantz, W. Lambert, P. Lindsey.
Packard Lepere LUSAC-11	1918	SC42133	• Acquired from Musée de l'Air. • Only one in existence.
SPAD S.XIII C.1		N2030A "16594"	
Standard J-1			• Uncovered, formerly Robert Greiger, Ohio.
Caproni Ca.36		2378	• On loan from Caproni Museum.
DH.4B		"S.63385"	• Was rebuilt from two originals. • Restored by Century Aviation. • Museum considers this a repro.
Avro 504k		1620 "D9029"	• Repro built in Canada from original parts.

Tulsa International Airport and Will Rogers Airport

Tulsa, OK, and Oklahoma City, OK

Type	Year	Serial number	Notes
(2) Parker Pushers (Curtiss type)			• Two Billy Parker planes were donated by Phillips Petroleum to Oklahoma airports.

Stafford Airport (Oklahoma)

Weatherford, OK

Type	Year	Serial number	Notes
Curtiss Pusher DIII	1911		• Flown by Eugene Ely.

Western Antique Airplane and Automobile Museum (WAAAM)

1600 Air Museum Road
Hood River, OR 97031

www.waaamuseum.org

Type	Year	Serial number	Notes
Curtiss JN-4D	1917	5137	• Retrieved from Ohio. • Restored by Terry Brandt/Tom Murphy.
Billy Parker Pusher	1910		• Rebuilt in 1934.

Evergreen Air and Space Museum

500 NE Captain Michael King Smith Way
McMinnville, OR 97128

www.evergreenmuseum.org

Type	Year	Serial number	Notes
DH.4	1918	3258	• "US Mail 166" • Used in many movies. • Is apparently airworthy. • Purchased by Collings Foundation in 2015 but may not move for a year.

Private Ownership (Michael Cilurso)

Allentown, PA

Type	Year	Serial number	Notes
Standard J-1			• Plane is apparently original and in need of restoration.

Golden Age Air Museum

371 Airport Road
Bethel, PA 19507

www.goldenageair.org

Type	Year	Serial number	Notes
Curtiss JN-4D	1918	8047	• "Daugherty" • Currently being restored. • Parts supplied by Byrd Mapoles, Milton, FL.

Eagles Mere Air Museum

Pennsylvania 42
Laporte, PA 17731

www.eaglesmereairmuseum.org

Type	Year	Serial number	Notes
Morane-Borel Monoplane	1910		• 50 percent original. • Personal plane of Mary De Forest Brush.
Polson Special (Racer)	1917		• Part of Denny Trone collection. • Formerly owned by Earl Daugherty.
Curtiss JN-4C	1917	c1122	• Formerly owned by Skeeter Carlson.
Thomas Morse Scout	1918	38898	• Formerly owned by Paul Mantz and later, Skeeter Carlson.

The Franklin Institute

222 N. Twentieth Street
Philadelphia, PA 19103

www.fi.edu

Type	Year	Serial number	Notes
Wright Flyer (B)	1911	No. 39	• Restored by Aeroplane Works, Carlisle, Ohio. • Formerly owned by Grover Cleveland Bergdoll.

Private Ownership (John Shue)

York, PA

Type	Year	Serial number	Notes
Curtis JN-4C		10875	• John Shue is a restorer of WACO aircraft.

The Frontiers of Flight Museum

Love Field
6911 Lemmon Avenue
Dallas, TX 75209

www.flightmuseum.com

Type	Year	Serial number	Notes
Curtiss JN-4D	1916	4072	• The plane was found leaning against a barn in New York in 1989. • It was restored by Danny Mintari.

Pioneer Flight Museum (Roger Freeman)

Old Kingsbury Aerodrome
190 Pershing Lane
Kingsbury, TX 78638

www.pioneerflightmuseum.org

Type	Year	Serial number	Notes
Thomas Morse Scout		38923	• Formerly owned by Tallmantz. • Owned by Freeman Heritage Collection, LLC.
Thomas Morse Scout			• Under restoration. • Both owned by Freeman Heritage Collection, LLC.
Curtiss JN-4 Canuck		c.308	• Being assembled from original parts.
Bristol F.2B			• One of the six in England used as roof trusses. • Possibly sold recently.

USAF Airman Heritage Museum

5206 George Avenue
Lackland Air Force Base, TX 78236

www.myairmanmuseum.org

Type	Year	Serial number	Notes
Curtiss JN-4D			• Fuselage only.

Pliska Display

Midland International Airport
9506 La Force Boulevard
Midland, TX 79706

Type	Year	Serial number	Notes
Pliska Biplane	1910		• Restored by EAA members in 1965.

Texas Air Museum

Stinson Field
1234 Ninety-Ninth Street
San Antonio, TX 78214

www.texasairmuseum.org

Type	Year	Serial number	Notes
Blériot Type	1912		• Owned by Katherine Stinson. • Only the engine is original.
Fokker D.VII			• Formerly at Rhinebeck, this is considered a replica but with an original airframe. • Aircraft may have been sold.

The Witte Museum

3801 Broadway Street
San Antonio, TX 78209

www.wittemuseum.org

Type	Year	Serial number	Notes
Curtiss JN-4D	1918	3805	• Formerly on loan to the Edward White II museum at Brooks AFB in San Antonio for thirty years, until the museum closed in 2011.

Museum of North Texas History

The Call Field Memorial at Kickapoo Airport
720 Indiana Avenue
Wichita Falls, TX 76301

Type	Year	Serial number	Notes
Curtiss JN-4D	1918	2525 "46"	• Formerly owned by Ray McWhorter, who was injured in a crash. • Stored in Burt, Iowa, barn for fifty years. • Found and restored by Dean Gilmore of Spencer, Iowa. • Restored again by Chet Peek in Norman, Oklahoma.

Hill Aerospace Museum

7961 Wardleigh Road
Hill AFB, UT 84056

www.aerospaceutah.org

Type	Year	Serial number	Notes
Curtiss JN-4D	1918	"5002" "43"	• Springfield built. • 90 percent original. • Found in 1957 by Jim Nissen in Oregon.

Blue Swallow Aircraft LLC (John Gaertner)

Earlysville, VA

www.blueswallowaircraft.com

Type	Year	Serial number	Notes
Curtiss JN-4D			• Restored and for sale. • Owned by a client of Blue Swallow.
Avro 504k	1925	A201	• Purchased from Stuart Tantrum's estate after his death. • It is all original in two crates, awaiting restoration.

Virginia Aviation Museum

5701 Huntsman Road
Richmond, VA 23250-2416

www.vam.smv.org

Type	Year	Serial number	Notes
Standard E-1	1918		• Formerly at Shannon Air Museum, this aircraft is one of two in existence.
SPAD S.VII	1917	B9913	• Apparently formerly owned by Jarrett. • Original parts from one plane. • Formerly in the Ricklef, Shannon Collection.

The National Museum of the Marine Corps

18900 Jefferson Davis Highway
Triangle, VA 22172

www.usmcmuseum.org

Type	Year	Serial number	Notes
DH.4	1918	102	• Formerly owned by Tallmantz. • Restored by Century Aviation.
Curtiss JN-4HG		4160	• Apparently a gunnery training version.
Thomas Morse S-4B			• Combination of an S-4C and an S-4B (two planes). • Officially considered a replica, with the fuselage going to Cradle of Aviation. The other 50 percent was restored by Century Aviation. • Apparently a kit plane from 1918 with fuselage three feet longer than it should be.

Military Aviation Museum

1341 Princess Anne Road
Virginia Beach, VA 23457

www.militaryaviationmuseum.org

Type	Year	Serial number	Notes
Curtiss JN-4D	1918	34135	• Formerly at Little Rock IMAX. • Restored in Argentina (aerohistoric.com). • Saint Louis–built Jenny.

The Wright Experience (Ken Hyde)

PO Box 3365
Warrenton, VA 20188

www.wrightexperience.com

Type	Year	Serial number	Notes
Burgess-Wright Model F	1911		• First aircraft to land at White House. • Flown from Boston to Washington, DC. • Original Wright vertical four engine No. 43. • Only example that exists. • Built by Starling Burgess of Marblehead, MA.
Curtiss JN-4D		386 "5361"	• Being restored for unnamed client.

National Postal Museum

2 Massachusetts Ave NE
Washington, DC 20002

www.postalmuseum.si.edu

Type	Year	Serial number	Notes
DH.4	1916	249	• Owned by NASM. • Formerly at San Diego Aero Museum. • Completely rebuilt in 1968 from six hundred pounds of pieces found at the crash site of a 1922 accident in Utah.
Wiseman-Cooke	1911		• Owned by NASM.

Smithsonian National Air and Space Museum

(Including the Steven F. Udvar-Hazy Center at Dulles Airport)
600 Independence Avenue SW
Washington, DC 20560

www.airandspace.si.edu

Type	Year	Serial number	Notes
Albatros D.Va	1917	D.7161/17	• "Stropp."
Caudron G.4	1917	C4263	
Curtiss JN-4D	1917	"4983"	
De Havilland DH.4	1918		• Used for experiments after the war.
Fokker D.VII	1918	4635/18 "U.10"	
Halberstadt CL.IV	1918		• Restored in Berlin.
Nieuport 28. C1	1919	"N4123A"	• Formerly at Rhinebeck.
Sopwith Snipe 7F1	1918		• Formerly at Rhinebeck.
SPAD S.XIII.C1	1918	"20"	• World War I pilot Ray Brooks' plane.
Standard J-1	1917		
Baldwin Red Devil	1911		• No engine. To be restored at Hazy.
Benoist Korn XII	1912	"32"	
Blériot XI	1911		• "Domenjoz." • Formerly at Rhinebeck.
Herring-Burgess	1910		
Curtiss D-III	1912		
Curtiss E	1913		• Boat hull only. • Formerly owned by Jack Villas.
Curtiss N-9H	1917		
Ecker Flying Boat	1913		
Felixstowe F5L	1918	A-3882	• Hull only.

Langley Aerodrome A	1903			
Langley Aerodrome 5 & 6	1896			
Lilienthal Standard	1894			
Montgomery Evergreen	1911		•	A glider.
Pfalz D.XII	1918			
SPAD S.XVI	1918	9392	•	Billy Mitchell's plane.
Voisin Type 8	1916	4640		
Wright Flyer	1903		•	Wright Flyer of Dec 17, 1903.
Wright Military Flyer	1909			
Wright "Vin Fiz"	1911			
Fowler Gage Biplane	1912			
Fokker T2	1922		•	Macready's plane.
Douglas World Cruiser	1921		•	"Chicago."
Sperry M-1 Messenger	1920	A.S.68533	•	Donated by Eddie Rickenbacker.
Martin Kitten KIII	1919		•	Unsuccessful high-altitude flyer.

Flying Heritage Collection (Paul Allen)

Paine Field, 3407 109th Street SW
Everett, WA 98204

www.flyingheritage.com

Type	Year	Serial number	Notes
Curtiss JN-4D	1918	3712	• "March Field" • Formerly owned by Ray Folsom, Roger Freeman.

Museum of Flight

9404 East Marginal Way S
Seattle, WA 98108

www.museumofflight.org

Type	Year	Serial number	Notes
Curtiss JN-4D	1917		• Museum states it's a partial replica.
Caproni Ca.20	1914		• Bought from Caproni Museum. • Kept unrestored. • Only one ever produced.
Aviatik DI	1918	101.40	• Formerly owned by the Berg family. • Bought in Europe by Art Williams.
Pfalz D.XII	1918	2848/18 (3498)	• Formerly owned by Tallmantz, Warner Bros., Balboni, Jarrett, and W&W.
Nieuport 28C1		donkey "14"	• Formerly owned by Jarrett and Tallmantz, by Bob Rust and Ned Kensinger. • Restored by Roger Freeman.

Seattle Museum of History and Industry

Museum of History and Industry (MOHAI)
PO Box 80816
Seattle, WA 98108

www.mohai.org

Type	Year	Serial number	Notes
Boeing Model 6 (B-1)	1919		• "US Mail"

The Columbia Gorge Interpretive Center Museum

990 Rock Creek Drive
Stevenson, WA 98648

www.columbiagorge.org

Type	Year	Serial number	Notes
Curtiss JN-4	1917		• Was lent to Pearson Air Museum (Vancouver, WA). • On loan from the Wally Olson estate.

EAA AirVenture Museum

3000 Poberezny Road
Oshkosh, WI 54902

www.eaa.org

Type	Year	Serial number	Notes
Curtiss JN-4D	1918	4904	• Formerly owned by Foster Hannaford Jr.
Curtiss E A-1 Pusher	1912	N24034	• Donated by Dale Crites in 1969.
Standard J-1	1917	1956 "N6948"	
Bates Tractor	1912		• On loan from Rich Colano, Burlington, Wisconsin.

SOUTH AMERICA

National Aeronautics Museum

Morón
Buenos Aires Province
ARGENTINA

Type	Year	Serial number		Notes
Ansaldo SVA 10		13164	•	In storage for future restoration.
Nieuport 28.C1			•	Just pieces from a crash, Lieutenant Matienzo.
Blériot XI			•	Used by Teodore Fels.
Balloon Basket			•	Used by Eduardo Newbery.

Aerospace Museum (Museu Aeroespacial)

Av. Marechal Fontenelle
2000-Campo dos Afonsos
Rio de Janeiro
BRAZIL

www2.fab.mil.br/musal

Type	Year	Serial number		Notes
Caudron G.3	1916		•	Formerly owned by Salis, W&W.
Nieuport 21 E1			•	Formerly owned by W & W.
			•	Called by some a reproduction.
			•	Apparently has a real engine, tail, and prop.

Aeronautical Museum of the Ecuadorian Air Force

Av. La prensa y Carlos V
Quito 593
ECUADOR

Type	Year	Serial number	Notes
Hanriot HD-1			• "TELEGRAFO 1" • Elia Liut, an Italian aviator, became the first man to fly across the Ecuadorian Andes.

Aeronautical Museum of Uruguay

Base Aérea Nº 1 Fuerza Aérea Uruguaya
Ruta 101 y Av. De Las Américas S/N
URUGUAY

www.artemercosur.org.uy/aeronautico

Type	Year	Serial number	Notes
Castaibert (type V 70 hp)			• Damaged in a recent fire.
Castaibert (type IV 80 hp)	1916		• Built in Argentina and used to train Uruguayan military pilots. • Also damaged in a museum fire.

Venezuela National AF Museum

Avendida Las Delicas
Avendida 19de Abril
Maracay, Aragua
VENEZUELA

Type	Year	Serial number	Notes
Caudron G.3	1919		• Said to be Venezuela's first military aircraft.

RUMORS...

Aircraft that may be where they are reported in these pages and perhaps are original, but have been difficult to verify.

Private Ownership (Major L. G. Hall)

Port Moresby
NEW GUINEA

Type	Year	Serial number	Notes
Curtiss Flying Boat			

Army Air Base Museum

Tokorozawa
JAPAN

Type	Year	Serial number	Notes
Salmson 2.A2			• Parts only?

El Ebane Military Headquarters Museum

Potosi
MEXICO

Type	Year	Serial number	Notes
Latino America	1916		

Santa Lucia Mexican AF Base

Santa Lucia
MEXICO

Type	Year	Serial number	Notes
GAF Type A	1916		

Aviation Museum of Melun Villaroche

Hangar Dayde Geumont, Aérodrome de Melun
77950 Montereau-sur-le-Jard
FRANCE

www.mamv.fr

Type	Year	Serial number	Notes
Hanriot Dupont HD14	1914		• Apparently being restored. • Could be counted twice with one at Le Bourget. • Was used for hunting.

Unknown Location

PERU

Type	Year	Serial number	Notes
Ansaldo SVA		"Cusco"	• Likely a replica.

VAF Technical School

Aragua
VENEZUELA

Type	Year	Serial number	Notes
Hanriot HD.1			

Estrella Warbirds Museum

4251 Dry Creek Road
Paso Robles, CA

www.ewarbirds.org

Type	Year	Serial number	Notes
Curtiss JN-4D	1918		• Owned by a museum member. • This aircraft belonged to William P. Clark, the former secretary of the interior. He kept it at the San Diego Air and Space Museum. It was scheduled to move to Estrella Warbirds Museum. Unfortunately, the plane was in the SDASM when it was consumed by fire. • Parts may survive somewhere.

Private Ownership (Jeff Hall)

Dayton, OH

Type	Year	Serial number	Notes
Thomas Morse Scout			• Formerly owned by Ray Watkins.
Curtiss JN-4D			• Crated since 1926. • Great shape—on sale for $200 thousand. • Formerly owned by Ray Watkins.
Blériot look-alike			• Formerly owned by Ray Watkins.

Unknown Location

United States

Type	Year	Serial number	Notes
Wright Model G Flying Boat	1913		• This is a 75 percent reconstructed original. • Last known discussion on the former Wrightseaplanebase.org.

Private Ownership (Neil Carr)

Unknown location

Type	Year	Serial number	Notes
Curtiss Thompson A-1 Pusher	1911		

Soukup and Thomas International Balloon and Airship Museum

(NOW CLOSED)

700 North Main Street
Mitchell, SD 57301

Type	Year	Serial number	Notes
Charles Dolfus Balloon Baskets	1890's		

Airpower Museum

22001 Bluegrass Road
Antique Airfield Route 2
Ottumwa, IA 52501

www.antiqueairfield.com

Type	Year	Serial number	Notes
Standard J-1	1917		• Possibly owned by John Desmond at one point.
Curtiss JN-4D			• It's not clear if either of these originals is at, or part of, Antique Airfield.

Bibliography: Journals, Catalogs, Books, Periodicals, Websites

Books:

Arango, Javier, Phillip Makann, Frank VanDersarl, and Jules VanDersarl. *The VanDersarl Blériot: A Centenary Celebration.* San Francisco, CA: Picturia Press, 2014.

Bowers, Peter M., and Ernest R. MacDowell. *Triplanes: A Pictorial History of the World's Triplanes and Multiplanes.* Osceola, WI: Motorbooks International, 1993.

Boyne, Walter J. *De Havilland DH.4: From Flaming Coffin to Living Legend.* Washington, DC: Smithsonian Institution Press, 1984.

Boyne, Walter J. *Fly Past, Fly Present: A Celebration of Preserved Aviation.* London: Arms and Armour, 1995.

Brooks-Pazmany, Kathleen L., and Claudia M. Oakes. *Aircraft of the National Air and Space Museum.* Washington, DC: Smithsonian, 1991.

Carisella, P. J., and James W. Ryan. *Who Killed the Red Baron? The Final Answer.* Wakefield, MA: Daedalus Pub., 1969.

Collections Catalog. *Owls Head Transportation Museum,* ME: Museum, 1988.

Elliott, Brian A. *Blériot: Herald of an Age.* Stroud, Gloucestershire, UK: Tempus, 2000.

Ellis, Ken. *Wrecks & Relics.* 20th ed. Hersham, Surrey, UK: Ian Allan Printing, 2006.

Faure, Marin. *Museum of Flight: 100 Years of Aviation History.* Seattle, WA: Elton-Wolf Pub., 2002.

Goodspeed, M. Hill, and E. Earle Rogers. *The Spirit of Naval Aviation: The National Museum of Naval Aviation.* Pensacola, FL: Naval Aviation Museum Foundation, 1997.

Gunston, Bill. *Giants of the Sky: The Biggest Aeroplanes of All Time.* Sparkford, Nr Yeovil, Somerset: Patrick Stephens, 1991.

Hallion, Richard. *The Rise of the Fighter Aircraft 1914–1918.* Annapolis, MD: N&A Publishing of America, 1984.

Hatch, Alden. *Glenn Curtiss: Pioneer of Aviation.* Guilford, CT: Lyons Press, 1942.

Hulls, John, and David Weitzman. *Rider in the Sky: How an American Cowboy Built England's First Airplane.* New York: Crown, 2003.

Hunt, Leslie. *Veteran and Vintage Aircraft.* New York: Charles Scribner's Sons, 1974.

Kelly, Fred C. *The Wright Brothers.* New York: Dover Publications, 1943.

Lamberton, W. M. *Fighter Aircraft of the 1914–1918 War.* Fallbrook, CA: Aero Publishers, Inc., 1960.

Larson, Erik. *Dead Wake: The Last Crossing of the Lusitania.* New York: Random House, 2015.

McCullough, David G. *The Wright Brothers.* New York: Simon & Schuster, 2015.

Molson, K. M., R. W. Bradford, and P. A. Hartman. *Canada's National Aviation Museum: Its History and Collections.* Ottawa: National Aviation Museum, 1988.

Munson, Kenneth. *Aircraft of World War I.* Garden City, NY: Doubleday, 1969.

Ogden, Bob. *Aviation Museums and Collections of Mainland Europe.* Hazelmere, Bucks: Air-Britain (Historians), 2006.

Opdycke, Leonard E. *French Aeroplanes before the Great War.* Atglen: Schiffer Pub., 1999.

Peek, Chester L. *Resurrection of a Jenny.* Norman, OK: Three Peaks Pub., 1994.

Pisano, Dominick. *Legend, Memory, and the Great War in the Air.* Seattle, WA: University of Washington Press, 1992.

Rimell, Ray. *World War One Survivors.* Bourne End, Bucks: Aston, 1990.

Roseberry, Cecil R. *Glenn Curtiss, Pioneer of Flight.* Syracuse, NY: Syracuse University Press, 1991.

Ross, John F. *Enduring Courage: Ace Pilot Eddie Rickenbacker and the Dawn of the Age of Speed.* New York: Saint Martin's Press, 2014.

Shaara, Jeff. *To the Last Man: A Novel of the First World War.* New York: Ballantine Books, 2004.

Stoff, Joshua. *Historic Aircraft and Spacecraft in the Cradle of Aviation Museum.* Mineola, NY: Dover Publications, 2001.

Tallman, Frank. *Flying the Old Planes.* Garden City, NY: Doubleday, 1973.

Taylor, John W. R., and Fred T. Jane. *Jane's Fighting Aircraft of World War I.* New York: Military Press, 1990.

Tillman, Barrett. *The Champlin Fighter Museum: Home of the American Fighter Aces Association and the J. Curtis Earl Automatic Weapons Collection.* Mesa, AZ: Aerofax, for Champlin Fighter Museum Press, 1991.

United States Air Force Museum. Wright-Patterson AFB, OH: Air Force Museum Foundation, 1985.

Welsh, George B. *San Diego Aerospace Museum: The Collection.* San Diego, CA: Museum, 1991.

Wohl, Robert. *A Passion for Wings, Aviation and the Western Imagination 1908–1918.* New Haven, CT: Yale University Press, 1994.

Journals/Magazines:

- *WW1 Aeroplanes*
- *Vintage Airplane*
- *Smithsonian Air & Space Magazine*
- *Aeroplane Magazine*
- *Cross & Cockade*
- *Over the Front*

Auction Catalogs:

- *The Norm Flayderman Collection of Vintage Aviation Memorabilia,* **Butterfield's**: November 14, 2000, in San Francisco, CA.
- *The S. F. Cody Archive,* **Sotheby's**: January 24, 1996, in London, UK.
- *Transport Memorabilia,* **Christie's**: February 1993, in South Kensington, UK.
- *The Contents of Wings & Wheels Museum,* **Christie's**: December 6, 1981, in Orlando, FL.

Websites:

www.anzacs.net
www.wingsofhistory.net
www.earlyaero.com
www.bristolaircraft.blogspot.com
www.jasta11.co.uk
www.collectors-edition.de
www.earlyaviators.com
www.wikipedia.org
www.barnstormers.com
www.crossandcockade.com

www.theaerodrome.com
www.wwiaviation.com
www.flyingmachines.org
www.earlyaeroplanes.com
www.tighar.org
www.warbirdinformationexchange.org
www.generalaviationnews.com
www.wrightexperience.com
www.riseofflight.com
www.warbirdsnews.com
www.wright-brothers.org
www.aeromedia.it
www.idflieg.com
www.airminded.org
www.century-of-flight.net
www.theaviationist.com
www.century-of-flight.net
www.avro504.org

Other Sources:

National Technical University of Ukraine (Kyiv Polytechnic Institute)

About the Author

Having lived in the New York metropolitan area all his life, Michael Antonelli has spent countless summer days wandering the quaint hangars of the Old Rhinebeck Aerodrome, enjoying the sights, sounds, and smells of early aviation. He has spent the better part of twenty years working for companies that specialize in compiling lists of US automobiles.

Michael has visited more than a hundred aviation museums throughout the United States, Canada, and Europe and has enjoyed documenting details of the early artifacts. Although familiar with many eras of flight, he concentrates on early aircraft and their history. The provenance of each original is of the greatest interest to him, much as it is to those who evaluate fine art or antiques.

Michael shares his passion for aviation's early history with his two children and wife of fifteen years.

He can be reached at **antonelli_michael@yahoo.com**.

Made in the USA
San Bernardino, CA
06 September 2017